"*Affirmations* bears the unmistakable voice of a pastor formed by faith, discipline, and deep love for God's people. Rooted in theological clarity and pastoral wisdom, these reflections speak with both conviction and compassion, offering readers guidance that is steady, thoughtful, and spiritually grounded. This work will serve pastors, ministry leaders, and thoughtful readers as a companion for reflection, encouragement, and faithful engagement with life's enduring questions."

—LAWRENCE C. HENRYHAND

Presiding Elder, Harrisburg District AME Churches

"Rev. Foley became far more than a local pastor; he functioned as a trusted bridge between clergy, government, healthcare institutions, and community organizations. I personally had the opportunity to attend numerous events where he partnered and provided leadership as a faith-based health justice pioneer, demonstrating his belief that spiritual ministry must also address physical and community well-being. His leadership extended across civic life as a founding leader of Black United Leadership in the Bronx (BULB), Police–Clergy Liaison for the 52nd Precinct, and advisory board member to institutions such as Montefiore Hospital, the American Cancer Society's Bronx Region, and the New York Yankees Community Relations Council. For nearly two decades, his partnership with Bronx Health REACH helped churches confront health disparities, diabetes and hypertension crises, food inequality, and systemic healthcare inequities, often using the pulpit itself to promote holistic health as an expression of Christian discipleship. It was therefore a profound honor, during my service as Council Member representing the community he faithfully served, to sponsor the co-naming of 'Pastor Robert Lewis Foley, Sr. Way,' ensuring that his legacy would remain permanently woven into the fabric of the Bronx."

—FERNANDO CABRERA

Senior Pastor, New Life Outreach International
and former New York City Councilman (2018–2021)

"*Affirmations: A Pastor's Reflections on Faith, Meaning, and Hope* reflects the thoughtful work of a pastor who clearly believed that faith must be examined with honesty and lived with integrity. Rev. Robert Lewis Foley Sr. writes out of decades of pastoral ministry, bringing together theological reflection and lived experience in the life of the church. These reflections reveal a minister who sought to discern the presence and purposes of God within the realities of human life. The book stands as a meaningful expression of pastoral theology shaped by faithful ministry."

—J. OSCAR MCCLOUD

Associate Pastor Emeritus, Fifth Avenue Presbyterian Church, New York City

"Timely, thoughtful, and deeply grounded, this work offers a compelling witness to the enduring relevance of pastoral theology at its best. *Affirmations* is both instructive and inspiring—a meaningful resource for readers seeking mature, honest, and hope-filled Christian reflection."

—SUSAN A. MENDOZA

Former Evangelist, Cosmopolitan Church of the Lord Jesus, Bronx, New York

Affirmations

Affirmations

A Pastor's Reflections on Faith, Meaning, and Hope

ROBERT L. FOLEY SR.

Edited and Compiled by
Robert L. Foley Jr.

Foreword by

J. Albert Bush Sr.

WIPF & STOCK · Eugene, Oregon

AFFIRMATIONS
A Pastor's Reflections on Faith, Meaning, and Hope

Wipf & Stock
An Imprint of Wipf and Stock Publishers
199 W. 8th Ave., Suite 3
Eugene, OR 97401

www.wipfandstock.com

PAPERBACK ISBN: 979-8-3852-7622-6
HARDCOVER ISBN: 979-8-3852-7623-3
EBOOK ISBN: 979-8-3852-7624-0

VERSION NUMBER 040226

All emphasis in Scripture quotations is the author's.

To the people of God:

This work is offered to the people of God as a word of encouragement along life's journey of faith. It is dedicated to all who seek to love God sincerely, to love others generously, and to walk with humility through the joys, challenges, and questions that shape our lives.

May these reflections serve as a companion in seasons of strength and uncertainty, inviting hearts to remain open to God's presence and attentive to the needs of others. May they encourage faith that is thoughtful, compassionate, and responsive to the spiritual and social concerns that touch our shared life.

Offered in the hope that, as we continue the journey together, we may be strengthened in faith, guided by love, and reminded that God meets us where we are and leads us forward with purpose and grace.

Contents

Foreword | xv

Preface | xix

SECTION I—FOUNDATIONS OF FAITH

Religion Defined | 3

Divine Worship: A Succinct Definition and Distinction from Religion | 4

Regarding the Purpose and Functions of Religion | 5

Regarding the Existence of God | 7

The Holiness of God | 9

The Righteousness of God | 10

Regarding the Old Testament | 11

Regarding Some Fallacies in the Bible | 14

Regarding the Bible as the Ultimate Source of the Word of God | 16

Regarding Goodness | 18

Regarding Evil | 20

Regarding Beliefs | 22

Regarding Faith | 23

A Clarification Regarding Philippians 4:13 | 25

Distinguishing Between Theology and Religion | 26

Contrasting Science and Theology | 27

Regarding Christian Theology | 28

Regarding the "Will" of God | 29

Regarding Christian Theism | 31

Distinguishing Between Belief and Faith | 33

Distinguishing Between Blessed and Bless-ed | 34

Regarding Myths | 35

The Doctrine of the Trinity | 36

In the Name of the Father, the Son, and the Holy Spirit | 37

Addendum: Two Additional Points to Consider | 39

Regarding Salvation | 40

SECTION II—THE PERSON AND WORK OF JESUS

Regarding Jesus as Preacher and Teacher | 43

Regarding Jesus as Redeemer | 44

Jesus Alone, Jesus Only: "The Leader of the Church" | 45

Jesus, the Embodiment of God's Grace | 48

I Am the Way, the Truth, and the Life | 51

I Am the Life | 52

Abide in Me | 53

Whose Disciple Are You? | 54

SECTION III—THE HUMAN CONDITION AND SPIRITUAL FORMATION

III.A — The Moral Struggle and Human Brokenness | 57

Regarding Obedience and Goodness | 57

Regarding Human Sinfulness | 58

Regarding the Fig Leaves of Adam and Eve | 59

Is a Clean Slate Possible? | 60

Regarding Forgiveness | 60

III.B — The Self: Identity, Consciousness, and Inner Life | 62

Regarding the Heart | 62

Regarding the "Soul-Self" | 62

Regarding the Loss of One's Soul | 64

Regarding the Location of My "Self" Before Its Association with My Body | 64
The Principle of Uncertainty | 66
III.C — The Body, Suffering, and Adversity | 68
Regarding the Body | 68
Regarding the Body (Additionally) | 69
Regarding Pain and Adversity | 70
Regarding Redemption and Redemptive Suffering | 70
Corrective Suffering | 71
Didactic Suffering | 71
Teleological Suffering | 71
Moral Suffering | 72
Healing Suffering | 72
Sacrificial Suffering | 72
Regarding Accidents | 73
Meaningful Presence in Ministry to the Terminally Ill | 75
III.D — The Nature of Evil, Judgment, and Divine Justice | 78
Regarding Possibility, Opportunity, and Evil | 78
Regarding a Quid Pro Quo Relationship with God? | 80
III.E — Metaphysical Questions: Life, Being, and Existence | 82
Regarding Life (What Is It?) | 82
Regarding the Meaning of Life | 82
III.F — Death, Eternity, and the Hope Beyond | 84
Regarding Death | 84
Regarding the Gates of Hell | 84
Regarding Heaven / Eternal Life | 85
The Problem of Hell and Additional Concerns Regarding Heaven | 87
Regarding Depression | 91

Regarding End-of-Life Choices (Particularly Suicide and Legal Euthanasia) | 97
Eternal Life, Its Mystery, and the Limits of Our Language | 97
Free Will in Eternity? | 99
III.G — Pastoral and Devotional Reflections | 101
I Believe | 101
Maintaining a Personal Journal of Poetry Through the Impacts of Existential Uncertainty and Anxiety | 102

SECTION IV—LOVE, EMOTION, AND MORAL CHARACTER

Regarding Love | 107
Agape — Its Meaning as I Understand It | 109
The Goal and Purpose of Love | 110
Another Thing About Love | 111
Love Never Fails Whom or What? | 112
Regarding Romance | 113
Regarding Jealousy | 114
Regarding Hatred | 116
Regarding Blessings | 117

SECTION V—SACRAMENTS, PRAYER, AND THE LIFE OF THE CHURCH

Regarding the Sacraments | 121
Regarding the Sacrament of Baptism | 123
Regarding "The Table of Grace" | 125
The Body and the Blood of Jesus | 126
Jesus' Exemplary Prayer Life | 127
Regarding Prayer | 129
Regarding Our Task as Preaching Theologians | 131
The Necessity of the Pastor? | 132
A Sermon Is a "Journey" | 133

SECTION VI—SOCIAL JUSTICE, CULTURE, AND CONTEMPORARY ISSUES

Regarding Power and Privilege | 137

Regarding Democracy as We Practice It | 138

Regarding the "Me Too Movement" | 140

Regarding Evangelicals in the United States | 142

Regarding the Murder at Emanuel AME Church—Continuing Violence and Murder in Our Nation | 144

Contemporary Church Dangers | 147

Regarding the Immanent Threat to Humanity | 148

SECTION VII—PHILOSOPHICAL REFLECTIONS AND MEDITATIVE PIECES

VII.A — Foundational Epistemology and Human Knowing | 153

Knowledge and Knowing | 153

VII.B — Self, Consciousness, and Human Being | 155

Regarding You and Me | 155

Regarding Consciousness and Self-Consciousness | 156

Regarding the Brain as the Receiver and Processor of Information | 157

VII.C — Reality, Existence, and Being | 159

Regarding Reality | 159

Regarding Nothingness: Is There Such a Thing? | 160

Regarding "Being" | 161

The Uniqueness of Our Uniqueness | 161

"That" I Am | 162

Regarding the Ground | 163

VII.D — Theological Explorations | 164

Where Did God Come From?—The Origin and the Emergence of God | 164

Some Inquiries Regarding Jesus | 166

Regarding Jesus, "The Son of Man" | 168
The Humanity and Divinity of Jesus | 168
Regarding God as the Creator of Jesus | 169
Is It God Can't or God Won't? | 169
God's Ultimate and Eternal Purposes | 170
VII.E — Meaning, Mortality, and Reflective Descent | 172
Where Are They? | 172
Imagine | 172
The Value of Quality Communication in Interpersonal Relationships | 174
The Contradiction of Belief | 174
Lending to the Lord? | 174

SECTION VIII—CALL TO ACTION
Just Thinking | 179
Still Just Looking Back or Looking Around and Ahead? | 180
Stuck in Self-Defeating Ways? | 181
Regarding Personal Opportunity | 183
Our Christian Witness and Its Future | 185
We Can and We Must Do Better | 188

SECTION IX—A SERMONIC WORD
STANDING IN NEED OF THE ULTIMATE AFFIRMATION | 195
The Epilogue | 201
Why Easter Matters to Me
Final Sermon Preached by Rev. Robert L. Foley Sr. — Easter Sunday, April 21, 2019 | 201

AFTERWORD | 207
A Tribute to the Reverend Robert Lewis Foley Sr. | 210

Appendix A: Hymns and Sacred Songs (Lyrics) Written by Rev. Robert L. Foley Sr. | 211

"Trusting in His Everlasting Words" | 211

"Worthy and Bless-ed Is He" | 212

Appendix B: Quotations | 213

Some of My Original Quotations | 213

More of My Original Quotations | 214

Foreword

As the California redwood stands tallest among other trees in the vast forest, so stood Rev. Dr. Robert L. Foley Sr., founder, and for many years pastor, of the Cosmopolitan Church of the Lord Jesus, Bronx, New York. A native of Marietta, Georgia, he was born, raised, and nurtured in the rich African Methodist Episcopal church tradition and was himself the son of an AME pastor, which grounded him solidly in the African American preaching tradition.

That grounding is important for understanding the spirit of this book. *Affirmations* is not merely a historical record of a pastor's ministry but a body of reflection shaped by a lifetime of preaching, study, pastoral care, and theological struggle. In these pages, readers will encounter a man seeking to speak with honesty and seriousness about God, faith, meaning, and the responsibilities of Christian discipleship.

Rev. Dr. Foley was a man who felt the Spirit of God tugging at the coattail of his imagination early in life, calling him to the ministry of the spoken word of God. It was a conviction that grew out of his personal experiences with the Civil Rights Movement of the 1950s and 1960s. He was greatly influenced by strong men like Martin Luther King Jr., Ralph David Abernathy, Julian Bond, Andrew Young, and many other prominent Civil Rights leaders of that era who dared to challenge the evils of segregation and Jim Crow, so prevalent across so much of landscape of the US, but especially in the Deep South.

Realizing that any serious call to Christian ministry is always preceded by the call to careful and prayerful study and preparation, Robert responded to "The Call" by preparing himself academically to meet the many and various challenges and demands associated with doing the ministry. He took his undergraduate degree from Morris Brown University in Atlanta, Georgia, and shortly thereafter took his first assignment as a pastor in the African Methodist Episcopal Church in the Georgia Conference in 1962. Determined to better ready himself to make a major dent in demolishing the walls of racism and discrimination so real in American society, Rev. Dr. Foley enrolled in Turner School of Theology at Interdenominational Theological Center in Atlanta, Georgia, in pursuit of the master of divinity degree, which he received in 1965. Later in life (2026), he went on to graduate with the doctor of ministry degree from Drew Theological Seminary in Madison, New Jersey.

In 1976, Rev. Dr. Foley was transferred to the New York Conference of the African Methodist Episcopal Church, where he served churches in Tuckahoe, New York, and in New York City. Meanwhile, he continued the work of fighting for justice and equality.

In 1978, Rev. Dr. Foley founded and organized what is now the Cosmopolitan Church of the Lord Jesus, an independent church serving the people of the Bronx, New York. Under his dynamic leadership the Cosmopolitan Church of the Lord Jesus became a beacon light to the people of this impoverished community. It was in this community that Rev. Dr. Foley identified with a people who yearned to "breathe free," which led him to take a leadership role in organizing and establishing the Faith-Based Outreach Initiative of what came to be known as Bronx Health REACH. This is where I first met and got to know Robert, through a lay member of my own congregation, Joyce H. Davis, herself a well-known community activist and builder.

As senior pastor of a leading Black Baptist Church in the Bronx, it was my pleasure to work alongside Rev. Dr. Foley in the building of Clergy Liaison for Bronx Health REACH. It was a very serious and fruitful effort to organize, empower, and engage local pastors and congregations across the denominational spectrum in an interfaith circle to bring meaningful and transformational change to the communities where we felt called to serve as ministers of the gospel. We challenged both clergy and laypersons in our community to speak up and speak out against the many evils that plagued our communities, such as disparities in the health care system, lack of affordable housing, substandard education, food insecurities, lack of teenage pregnancy care and prevention, and a host of other societal ills prevalent in marginalized communities.

What makes this especially significant is that Rev. Dr. Foley did not separate theological reflection from lived discipleship. He understood that Christian thought must bear upon the actual burdens of human life. That same conviction is evident throughout *Affirmations*, where matters of doctrine, moral responsibility, suffering, and hope are never treated as abstractions alone but as realities bound up with the life of persons and communities.

The affirmations contained in this book reflect the theological convictions that undergirded the ministry of Rev. Dr. Foley and informed the preaching he shared with his congregation at the Cosmopolitan Church of the Lord Jesus during his forty-year tenure as pastor. Because he was a man of deep and abiding faith, he always sought to address the challenges of his day in the style and tradition of the great prophets of the Old Testament—like Moses, Elijah, Jeremiah, Isaiah, Ezekiel, Amos, and Nehemiah—and, of course, in the style of the Chief Shepherd of the church, Jesus Christ. Rev. Dr. Foley's preaching was always filled with both passion and compassion. As a preacher of the gospel, he never failed to speak truth to power, and he was never afraid to challenge the status quo.

Readers of this book will also discover another dimension of Rev. Dr. Foley's voice: not only his prophetic urgency but his disciplined effort to define terms carefully, examine inherited assumptions, and press for greater clarity in Christian teaching. He was concerned that faith should not rest on careless language or shallow repetition but on thoughtful reflection, moral seriousness, and a sincere pursuit of truth.

Affirmations: A Pastor's Reflections on Faith, Meaning, and Hope is a book of affirmations and pastoral-theological reflections arising from the mind, heart, and ministry of a seasoned pastor. It invites pastors, teachers, students, church leaders, and thoughtful believers to engage a serious body of work that wrestles with the meaning of faith, the demands of discipleship, the challenge of suffering, and the calling of the church in the world. As you read these powerful affirmations and reflections, you are certain to detect the voice of a twenty-first-century prophet addressing the challenges of his own day while also comforting the people entrusted to his pastoral care. After reading these affirmations, you will discover that Rev. Dr. Foley understood that in order to preach the gospel faithfully, one must be willing and able to both comfort the afflicted and to afflict the comfortable—at the same time. In these affirmations, you will hear both compassion for the needy and the prophetic call to action that marked Rev. Dr. Foley's ministry. Rev. Dr. Foley firmly believed that authentic faith must be accompanied by serious action on the part of both the oppressed and the oppressor. For Rev. Dr. Foley, faith and action are inextricably bound together, and "what God has joined together, let not man [or woman] separate" (Mark 10:9 KJV).

Dr. J. Albert Bush Sr.
Senior Pastor, Walker Memorial Baptist Church, Bronx, New York

Preface

By the grace and favor of God, I have been privileged to preach the gospel of Jesus and the whole Counsel of God as revealed to me for more than sixty years. I have also been privileged to serve as the pastor of eight congregations in Georgia and New York over the past fifty-six years.

Many of those years were spent preaching and teaching the orthodox positions of the Christian church, the scholarly insight of many theologians whose teachings informed and inspired me early on but also challenged me *not* to ultimately rest my affirmations and "my truth" solely upon their teachings and scholarly presentation in support of the "truths" insisted upon by the creeds, the doctrines and traditions of the church, and the content of much of the kerygma so familiar and routine, so frequently affirmed and espoused by preachers and teachers in the churches and through broadcast and print media.

I have struggled across the years with what I perceived to be some seriously inadequate or misleading interpretations of Scriptures, the meaning of the sacraments, and the meaning of much of our Christian vocabulary. I confess that I once routinely preached and adhered to much that is still orthodox and traditional doctrine and interpretations of Scripture that I now consider to be misinformation and, in some instances, disinformation because it was and is misleading, self-contradictory, inconsistent, and some of it even manipulative so as to strengthen the authority of the church and the power of the clergy.

At some point in my life, however, I reached the conclusion that much of what has been preached and taught by too many persons across the years *was* and *is* still lacking significant clarity and even honesty, to a large extent, because most preachers are conditioned to routinely proclaim and teach the traditional views that are so familiar to persons who are or would be Christians without the specificity and clarity that facilitates the clearest and most reliable understanding that is necessary and empowered to inspire the quality of confidence that can enable a person to make existential decisions and commitments in the context of Christian religion.

We cannot continue to do this. If we want the church (Christian men, women, and children) to have the best opportunity to be secure in their knowledge, to evangelize, and to more effectively and persuasively reach the millions in the United States and throughout the world who sincerely desire to follow Jesus, we cannot continue hindering them by the lack of clarity, the contradictions, the faulty interpretations, and the misleading that has been woven into the fabric of much of our preaching and teaching.

We can do better and we must do better. We are living in what some today call "The Information Age." Most people in the United States, in particular, and many in the world at large have access to the internet where they can "fact check" unlimited information. More and more people today, therefore, do not consider it to be important, meaningful, or necessary to be a part of organized religion or to sit in a church on Sunday to hear an unclear, unexceptional, and unfathomable message that makes no sense to them when they can do their own research in their quest for biblical coherence and *truth*.

It concerns me that the focus of much of our preaching and teaching inclines people to focus on how to receive a blessing as opposed to finding that path that enables one to be a blessing and to live a blessed life. It concerns me that we have not found the courage to acknowledge that there are some contradictions and some inconsistences in all translations of the Bible and that the Bible itself is a great book, a wonderful book, a book like no other but it is *not* a perfect book. God did not make a perfect people. The author of the book of Genesis declares that with reference to most of the realizations from God's creative genius. God said "that's good" and not "that's perfect."

It is extremely difficult for me to see where God has produced anything utilizing human involvement or assistance that is perfect. Perfect means perfect—that is, no blemishes, no inconsistencies, no contradictions, no incompleteness, no disharmony, and no errors.

The Bible is the best book we presently have in our search to more clearly understand God, and to discover God's truths, but it is not perfect historically, geologically, factually, logically, or grammatically at every single point. Some of the teachings in the Old Testament were even rejected by Jesus as impractical and untenable. For example, His rejection of "an eye for eye." We see it evidenced again and again when He justified "harvesting on the Sabbath in some instances."

The Bible is not a perfect book, but when we take care and do our best to properly and honestly interpret it, it is the best spiritual resource we currently have in print today. Jesus never said that the Torah, the psalms, or the prophetic books of the Old Testament would lead or guide the disciples and us into the realizations of the truth about God or His teachings. Jesus said the Holy Spirit would help us to achieve that.

As wonderful and uniquely informing as the Bible is, it's value and meaningfulness is contingent upon the quality of our thoughtful analysis and our interpretations. I believe we must make a continuous and sincere effort at all times to courageously and unapologetically strive to be honest, follow the evidence wherever it leads, and more clearly define what is meant by what we proclaim if our preaching and teaching is to be respected as honest and as assuring or reassuring as it can be and should be to all who dare to trust us as authentic spokesperson's for God and Jesus.

Dr. Edgar Sheffield Brightman, a distinguished philosopher and theologian, once compared religion without thought to a boat used without a rudder. I agree. Our knowledge and insight derived from the Bible, the Holy Spirit, and trustworthy, qualitative resources that are more likely than less likely enablers of the realization of truth should enable those who listen to our teaching and preaching to realize within themselves the more likely clarity and truth that inspires more meaningful understanding, confidence, deeper commitment, and devotion as followers of "the way" that is revealed to us through Jesus.

Perhaps you are wondering what *truth* is to me. I hold that truth is the most reliable information that you can possibly have regarding any particular thing that concerns you at any particular time.

I do not expect for my affirmations herein to be convincing to all who become acquainted with them. I do not expect all persons to agree with them or to affirm them. I do hope, however, that many will be moved to reevaluate and reconsider what *they* mean by their own affirmations and then decide what seems to be more likely or less likely the truth. We must at all times follow the evidence where it leads.

Manuscript and writings by

Rev. Robert Lewis Foley Sr., MDiv, DMin, DD

SECTION I

FOUNDATIONS OF FAITH

Religion Defined

True religion is the theological, spiritual, and moral perspective—and the accompanying affirmations—that establish, inform, guide, and govern one's value judgments, choices, and decisions and ultimately shape one's way of life at all times, in all conditions and circumstances.

Restated:

True religion concerns the theological, spiritual, and moral beliefs and perspectives that inform, instruct, propel, and guide a person's affirmations, actions, and behaviors in all situations, conditions, and circumstances. True religion, therefore, is to be understood as the decisive factor in how and why a person lives his or her life at all times.

Divine Worship: A Succinct Definition and Distinction from Religion

Divine worship is a celebration of the majesty of God through appropriate ceremonies, rituals, protocols, and other words of praise, sung or spoken and dedicated to God with a joyful spirit of thanksgiving and respect.

Divine worship, although inclusive of religious content, is not "religion." Simply put, divine worship is a celebration of what one claims to believe and value concerning God.

Religion is the way of living that one sincerely attempts to fulfill at all times, in all conditions and circumstances, guided by what one believes and values as prescribed, instructed, or inspired by God.

Regarding the Purpose and Functions of Religion

The *goal of religion* is to set us (the believers) on the path that, if faithfully adhered to, will provide the best opportunity for us to realize harmony with God. That is extremely important because harmony with God provides for blessings within our consciousness that are not material but a quality of peace, joy, security, and well-being that will endure forever. The excitement and satisfaction that we derive from money, food, and material things will pass away, but the blessings derived from the realization of harmony with God are in themselves eternal.

The *functions of religion*, therefore, are as follows:

1. To help us discover and gain significant clarity regarding the meaning of life and its mysteries, the reasons for our existence, and our purpose and function as seen from the perspective of God
2. To keep us properly focused regarding the importance of thinking and living the quality of life that helps us to facilitate and maintain a harmonious relationship with God
3. To give us confidence as we journey through this life that we never journey alone—that God does love and care for us and is with us at all times
4. To enable us to freely embrace the values taught to us by *Jesus* such as love, kindness, compassion, forgiveness, and service to others that reflects our concern for their well-being
5. To increase within our self-consciousness our deepest and most abiding sense of personal value by giving to us the understanding that we are living for a purpose and a cause in cooperation with God that is more meaningful and more enduring than our ego-satisfying aspirations such as great wealth, power, and popularity

6. To help us make choices and decisions that contribute toward the realization of sustainable moral character, thereby enabling us to behold ourselves in the image and likeness of God
7. To provide us with powerful and resourceful gifts:
    - *Love*, which gives to us our most profound sense of personal worth and value
    - *Beliefs*, which establish what we hold to be trustworthy and true
    - *Faith*, which is not *what* we believe but how we actually live and what we do at all times consistent with what we claim to believe
    - *Hope*, which is that resource within ourselves that gives to us enduring optimism regarding the favorable outcomes we desire or expect concerning whatever concerns us

Regarding the Existence of God

I do not think of God in the context of existence. I do not refer to God as existing. Existence, to me, implies that something or someone is or should be perceptible to one or more of our senses or our direct observation in some way. Therefore, I say no, God does not exist. God "is." I add to that: "God is real," and "God has always been and always will be."

Furthermore, God is not "a" anything. God is *the*, God is *our*, God is *your*, God is *my*, but God is not "anything." God is not a father; God is our Father. God is not a spirit; God is the eternal spirit. God is not a rock in a weary land; God is *my* rock and, hopefully, *your* rock in a weary land. God is not a creator; God is *the* Creator, *your* Creator, *our* Creator, and *my* Creator, and so on.

Some linguists, etymologists, and others may consider the distinction I make here more tautology or a matter of personal preference. But if we are concerned to convey meaning that is clearly understood we must consider how the "man in the street" is more likely to understand what we mean by what we say. I contend that to "the man in the street," the words *exist* and have *real* connotations that extend beyond the definitions and denotations in the various lexicons.

The man in the street can understand the expression that "love is real" but not a reference that love exists or joy exists or truth exists or that a surprise exists. To the "man in the street," those kinds of experiences are real, but they do not have corporeal, physical, or material presence or existence. Their effect or their impact does make the case that they *are real*, but they do not *exist*.

Many particular nonmaterial/nonphysical experiences, thoughts, and feelings I have do not exist to me, but they are realized by me, known to me, and are important to me, but they are not known and are not capable of being experienced by others in the same way. They often have value to me not because they have existence as such but because they *are real* to me and have function, effect, meaning, and purpose to me.

I earnestly believe that the "man in the street" has a natural tendency to think that if someone or something *exists*, they or it *should be* perceptible to our senses or capable of being observed in some way. That is not true regarding all things considered to be *real*. How we speak about God and make references to God in our words spoken, written, or signed does *matter*. God is *real*. To me, the things we denote as existing are finite, but that which is real is infinite.

The Holiness of God

The word *holy* literally means "separate" or "separated" or "set apart." Some may include words such as "special," "uncommon," "revered," or "praiseworthy" in an effort to describe what the holy is. It is, to be sure, a perspective that a person may have regarding someone or something that is respectfully considered to be "one of a kind" or a "one and only" and therefore worthy of our best response, including but not limited to our respect, our admiration, our devotion, and our care.

Holiness, therefore, is not a part of the character of God; it is a reference to the position that God occupies in the "hearts and minds" or the perspective of all who consider God to be holy. This is to say that God is Holy because of the uniquely high regard and respect that believers have for God, and it is concretized by their trust and confidence in God's love, God's power, and God's character (i.e., God's righteousness and goodness).

To say that God is Holy is not to merely say that God is different or that God is "other" than ourselves but that God is different and other than ourselves for very specific reasons that include the evidences or one's beliefs concerning God's eternal love and care for all creation, God's unique abilities, God's unique character, God's goodwill, and God's unique goals and purposes.

The Righteousness of God

The righteousness of God is a reference to the unchanging flawless character of God and the everlasting commitment of God to the moral values that God affirms as intrinsically good and that God instructs us to uphold in our thoughts, our decisions, and our behaviors. The righteousness of God is also a reference to God's absolute unwillingness to practice, encourage, support, or cooperate with evil. Evil, of course, is anything and everything that opposes, undermines, or contrasts the intrinsic moral values affirmed by God.

The righteousness of God is the assurance that there are moral values that are vital to the realization of the eternal purposes of God. The righteousness of God is God's guarantee that *good* will ultimately prevail over evil not only here on earth but throughout the universe and throughout the ultimate realization that Christians call heaven.

Goodness and evil, or "the positive value and its opposite" have always been possible as concepts, but God is the one who actualized "the good," and as a consequence, its opposite necessarily emerged as a concrete presence in the universe as a matter of function in the dynamic of "moral freedom and choice" by persons.

God was not *bound* or *limited* by forces or powers beyond God's self that restricted God. God was free to choose to be other than what God was and is and to do other than what God chose or chooses to do. God, however, circumscribed God's self (or as some would say Himself). It was when God freely chose to eternally affirm and commit "God's self" to "the good" as the value that best compliments God's (His) eternal goals and purposes and gives to all persons and the universe itself the best opportunity for enduring well-being, that "the good" was clearly and decisively "actualized" as the essential structure in the formation of the character of God.

Regarding the Old Testament

The Old Testament is primarily a theological history of the Hebrews, also subsequently known as the Israelites and the Jews. This history is inclusive of their views regarding the origins of the universe and its contents, the creative and governing power in the universe (God), their religious beliefs, their legal, moral, and ethical codes, their cultural and political development, their nation-building initiatives, their poetry, and their understanding of why things are as they are.

In the Old Testament Scriptures, it is proclaimed that the one true God initiated and entered into an agreement with Abraham, assuring Abraham that if he, his descendants, and his community would faithfully submit to God's divine leadership and instruction, they would be blessed with God's "most special favor" and would, thereby, prosper and grow into a great community (nation or kingdom) that would be a blessing to all other nations and endure forever.

Interestingly, upon honest and objective examination and analysis, it is clear that the Old Testament often presented or described God in ways that are troubling. To cite a few for example, in the Old Testament, God is sometimes portrayed as good and merciful and at other times vindictive and prone to violence in God's effort to solve problems or to accomplish God's will.

Additionally, God is at times portrayed as an advocate for peace and at other times the instigator of war. Still, at other times God is portrayed as a lover of "His people" but being displeased with them for assorted reasons, they assert that God inspired or motivated other nations to overcome them through military engagement and/or to take them into captivity.

Those misguided notions can be attributed to flaws in their theology and in their worldview perspective at a time when most religious people along with the Jews believed that God was the "cause of all things," and no matter how much pain, discomfort, or destruction any action or event caused, to them *God did it* because it satisfied God in some way and was therefore consistent with what they understood to be the prerogative of a just and righteous God.

Although some of the flaws in their theology are astoundingly contradictory and so apparent, particularly concerning the behavior of God, and even though many persons disregard or excuse the flawed limitations of their theology and their worldview, it is suggested here that the contradictions presented cannot justifiably be excused, upheld, or defended.

It surely seems that God has constructed the world and indeed the universe in ways that provide for and accommodate the "freedom of the individual and individuals" to make their own choices and decisions and to activate them within the confines of their opportunities and their ability. This clearly suggests that the "freedom of each individual," competent and able enough to freely choose and decide for themselves is of supreme importance to God. God simply does not *control* and does not desire to *control* the thoughts, the choices, the decisions, or the actions of any person. Does God endeavor to lead or influence persons? The answer is yes but not through direct *control.*

God has made persons free to do as they please but with the understanding that the abuse or misuse of one's freedom of will, from time to time, generates built-in or concomitant consequences that will be hurtful to one's self and others as well. If God were to "puppetize" and "roboticize" each and every individual person, thus denying them personal freedom, God would then be in total control and, therefore, directly responsible for all wars, all injustice, and everything both bad and good concerning all things that human beings do.

God, however, does not desire to control individuals, communities, or our nations. God does desire for all persons to *freely* embrace, affirm, and live the moral values and ethics emanating from God's own righteousness that can enable each person to *freely* uphold the *right* and the *good* and thereby obtain the genuine and authentic character that enables them to *freely* realize harmonious relations with God and other persons with God's leadership, instruction, and influence but without God's control, force, or coercion.

Many authors or contributors to the books of the Old Testament especially were greatly influenced by the prevailing "worldview" of their day and by certain cultural pressures and opinions in their communities that made it quite easy for them to interpret or portray God with some flawed views that distorted their message both then and now. In too many instances, God was presented by them to the community as good and merciful *sometimes*, only to seemingly deny or contradict it on other occasions by presenting God to the community as an impatient, intolerant, vengeful, bloodthirsty executioner and murdering tyrant. That is the image of a "god" difficult to love, respect, and trust with all one's heart. That is the god who is not the one God, and even if that god were real, that god could not possibly be embraced as "Our Father."

There is a popular saying often heard in the worship services of Black congregations; it conveys the view that "God is good all the time, and all the time God is good." If God directly controlled all, most, or just some of the decisions and actions of persons, that saying referenced above would be inaccurate and untrue. Individuals and communities of persons are good sometimes and sometimes evil. That is *never* the case with God no matter who says otherwise.

Many times, in an effort to avoid or to escape responsibility and accountability for their immoral or evil behaviors, individuals and communities "take God's name in vain" by thinking and claiming that God is in control and consequently responsible. God, however, will not do anything inconsistent with God's character which is God's righteousness, and God will not do what God has instructed or expects for us not to do.

Regarding Some Fallacies in the Bible

Some of the Old Testament is fallacious but certainly not all. It contains and conveys some, and in certain texts, it presents or describes the thoughts and actions of God in ways that are troubling. As I indicated in the first part of my document regarding the Old Testament, we must be clear that the Old Testament is a *particular* history of the Hebrews/Israelites/Jews. What makes it both particular and peculiar is that it represents their attempt to set forth (to explain or describe) their history from a predominantly theological perspective through their patriarchs, sages, priests, prophets, and charismatics (such as Joshua, David, and Solomon). That alone makes their presentation of their history particularly unique. It is their attempt to describe their origins, their journey, and their experiences in the world from a theological perspective rather than a political, sociological, and/or anthropological perspective.

The greatest flaws in their theology were generated by their insistence that they were God's "chosen people," and this gave them cover to say and do as they please (and they did attempt to say and do as they please). That thinking and that inclination has not diminished even to this day, even though the contemporary nation of Israel is more political, sociological, and even more militaristic but less theological in their self-understanding and discourse.

Simply put, some of the Old Testament theology is flawed because of the aggressive attempt by the authors and editors of the Old Testament to occasionally but quite notably take God's name in vain in the effort to explain themselves especially with reference to more than a few of their violent and cruel military campaigns and actions. The Hebrews, as presented in the Old Testament, were the original "God Is on Our Side Chorus." (The United States has mimicked and still mimics that same chorus from time to time.)

It is appropriate and right to affirm that in spite of its flaws at various times and in various settings, the "Word of God" still breaks through, and if we do not allow ourselves to become deluded and misled by SOME of their flawed theological assumptions, God's character and God's truth still breaks through. We must read and preach and teach God's "alleged" and questionable actions and proclamations in the clarifying light of what Jesus has to say about God.

Some of the prophets, to be sure, and maybe even many of the prophets challenged the "theologically based ethnocentric excesses" that governed the thinking of their own Hebrew ancestors and some of their contemporaries regarding their self-understandings and their "taking the name of God in vain assumptions."

The major theological flaws in the Old Testament are attached to the Hebrews' view of themselves as God's chosen people, which undergirded their vicious and brutal hegemony goals and their view of God as vengeful and, therefore, their avenger. Even David, who often spoke of God as loving, kind, and full of mercy in one moment would, in the next moment, brag about how God defeated (slaughtered or destroyed) his (David's) perceived enemies.

To all of that Jesus says, "Nonsense." Jesus proclaims that God is the Father of all and the Father who does not take the side of any man or woman, nor any family, community, or nation. Jesus instructs us that our Father is on the side of whoever and whatever gives to *all* persons the best opportunity and means to realize well-being and to assist the process that is intended to enable all persons to become representative of the image and likeness of God. They are the ones who live and labor to advance the realization of the Kingdom of God, where all people live in harmony with God and with one another and are eternally committed to the will, the goal, and the purposes of God.

Regarding the Bible as the Ultimate Source of the Word of God

Without question, the Bible is, and deservedly so, the most revealing, profound, informative, and inspiring document we *presently have* concerning God. The Bible is the clearest and the most convincing resource we *presently have today in print* that conveys so much that is needed as we consider and reflect upon the personality of God, the character of God, the activity of God, the love of God, the purposes of God, and God's truth.

It is, however, mistaken and misleading to assume or suggest that God has limited or restricted all revelations of the God-self to humanity through the *present Bible* alone. It is inconceivable, moreover, that a truly thoughtful and reasonable person today or ever would conclude that *any one book* could possibly contain, reveal, or express all that God is, all that God has to say, and all that God may do and will do in the free exercise of God's prerogatives from this day forward and forever.

God is still speaking and revealing the God-self and will continue doing so as God addresses and processes the myriads of problems, needs, aspirations, failures, changes, and challenges that impact humanity billions of years from today and in worlds far different from this present world. This, of course, assumes that what we today call "human beings" will still exist in some form or expression.

If human beings are still existing going forward, there will be billions upon billions and trillions upon trillions of issues, cares, and concerns that humanity will have to struggle with that the *present Bible* does not and cannot include within its scope. Although many issues that humanity has struggled with since the beginning of human history still impact humans today, we must come to understand that advances in science and technology in particular are changing many things that concern us, and fast. Science and technology are changing our understanding of the world in which we live and operate, changing our understanding of who and what we are, changing our understanding of the universe, and changing our understanding of what we mean by concepts such as *life, a person, relationship, family, love, you, me, marriage, up, down, time, God, value, truth,* and so on.

To be sure, neither we nor our best minds can even begin to conceive the full implications and ramifications of how computerization, artificial intelligence, robotics, the colonization of distant planets, global warming, nuclear warfare, cellular mutations, and genetic manipulation and disturbances will impact humanity and planet Earth going forward. Additionally, we cannot presently conceive the implications and/or the consequences of the certain discovery of other nonhuman intelligent beings and other life forms in this universe, and the realization that there are other universes.

Even then, God will continue to speak and reveal the God-self but in ways that the *present Bible* does not and cannot. Yet, *the Bible is still the best source and resource* that we presently have concerning God and the nature of our relationship/connection with God as revealed by God. We would do well to remember, however, the words of the poet who said, "God moves in a mysterious way; His wonders to perform."[1] Take notice that the poet did not say God has moved or God used to move in a mysterious way. He informs us in this declaration that God initiates, responds, adjusts, and speaks regarding changing times, conditions, issues, discoveries, challenges, and so on in unique, creative, purposeful, unpredictable, often unintelligible ways and will continue to do so until the end of time and throughout eternity. God is the ultimate source of God's *Word*. God still speaks and always will speak to humanity above and beyond the pages of any one book and all books combined, no matter how numerous.

1. William Cowper, "God Moves in a Mysterious Way" (1773).

Regarding Goodness

Goodness as a particular moral quality is a value and standard that can only be freely realized, obtained, and actualized in a person's thoughts and behaviors and cannot ever be realized or obtained or actualized by compulsion or force.

A legal mandate or requirement to act or not to act in a certain way can be compelled and forced by the police, the judicial and regulatory authority of the government, but the realization of respect or appreciation for that mandate or requirement by a person cannot be compelled or forced by threats of fines, seizure of property, imprisonment, or death. Moreover, compliance with any mandate or requirement only because of force or the fear of possible adverse consequences if one does or does not comply cannot be considered "good."

The "wellsprings" for the concept of goodness can come from a variety of sources but only as concepts. The motivation for actual commitment to the concepts of goodness that we practice or act upon, however, must be inspired by God within the person and freely chosen by the person as foundational to his or her way of life. God can and does *inspire* and *motivate* persons toward the realization and the achievement of goodness, but God will not impose it. If God imposed moral goodness upon a person, the realization of an authentic and genuine moral character of a person would not be possible. Each person is solely responsible and accountable for their moral choices and behaviors.

Goodness is always affirming of what operates to facilitate harmony with God and others, and to support and provide for the well-being not only of one's self but all other people too. Be clear and certain that not all goodness is legal, and not all that is legal is intrinsically or purposefully good.

Simply stated, *goodness* is the moral value or quality that upholds, sustains, and undergirds the meaning, goal, and purpose of all the other positive values that are intended to operate universally (without individual exception) in the best interests and towards the well-being of one's self and all persons including, first and foremost, God.

Regarding Evil

God did not create evil. Evil was always a possibility that emerged as a reality when God decided to create human beings who would be morally free and capable of making their own choices and decisions through the empowerment of free will.

God could have created human beings without the empowerment of free will. But this would have resulted in the subjugation of human beings to God's absolute dictates and control. Under that arrangement, a human being could not possibly become a true "self" and could not possibly realize the quality of authentic and genuine "goodness and character."

Free will is absolutely essential and necessary in an environment where authentic choices and decisions can be made by a person and acted upon by that person. If a person does not have choices and alternatives, moral freedom is not possible.

God is eternally aligned with "the good" and with righteousness, which are key to the fulfillment of God's ultimate and eternal purposes. Evil, recognizing that human beings have moral freedom, fully intends to dominate human beings, this world, and probably the universe. God, however, fully intends to prevent evil's domination but not at the expense of the abrogation of the free will that God has given to human beings. *Without the reality of free will,* authentic and genuine love, character, righteousness, and goodness cannot be realized, respected, or appreciated by God or any person.

The abuse and misuse of the free will that God has given human beings is the overwhelming cause of God's "heartaches and sadness" and much of the heartache and suffering of human beings. God could end that right now, and evil along with it, if only God would deny human beings free will and transform us into puppets or slaves. Thus far God has refused to do so, and it is not likely that God will ever destroy the empowerment of free will that has been given to human beings.

It is important to clearly understand that there is a difference between evil and adversity and between evil and misfortune. Natural disasters and accidents are unfortunate but not necessarily evil. Evil has connotations that require the cooperation and facilitating actions by a person who is capable of making moral decisions and judgments.

Evil has no power to direct or control the actions, the thoughts, or the behaviors of any person capable of making moral judgments and decisions until they submit and cooperate with it. Evil cannot force itself and its objectives on anyone. Evil allures, tempts, invites, and often persuades persons to cooperate with it. Evil, however, has no dominating or controlling power over anyone who refuses to cooperate with it.

Regarding Beliefs

A belief is an *assumption*, and a believer is a person who accepts the validity of the assumption. Just because a belief is an assumption, however, does not mean that it is just a whim. A whim is the realization of either an idea, impulse, notion, or dream that usually and suddenly appears in a person's mind without significant aforethought and reason.

A belief is an assumption that requires some deliberate forethought and some reasons in support of the belief that validates it, in the mind of the believer, as reasonable and true. In essence, there are some persuasive and convincing reasons that undergird the assumptions of all believers.

It is important for the believer to analyze his or her beliefs periodically. To the best of their ability, they must try to determine honestly and objectively what is more likely or less likely the case concerning the content and validity of their beliefs.

Regarding Faith

Faith should not be understood as a synonym for belief because faith is more than believing. Faith is a commitment to what one professes to believe and is made evident by the actions and activities that accompany that commitment. A person, therefore, does not literally "have" or possess faith, a person "has" beliefs that can become the foundation or the basis of or for their activity and actions that we should understand to be *faith*.

Beliefs can be held by a person without action or activity, but faith cannot because *faith is the activity* and *the action* that are the evidences of what a person believes.

To further expand and clarify, faith is "works and action" done by a person that are informed and guided by what one confidently claims or professes to believe as trustworthy and worthy of one's commitment. A careful reading and thoughtful reflection regarding how the word *faith* is used in the Bible clearly suggests that faith is not only a noun but a verb—because faith is what one actually "does," having everything to do with what one believes.

Consider Jesus' response to the woman with the issue of blood. Jesus said to her, "Your faith has made you whole" (see Matt 9:20–24). It can be correctly paraphrased to say, "Your actions today in support of what you believe have served to facilitate your healing."

Consider also some verses from Hebrews, chapter 11, in this light:

Because Abraham believed, because Abel believed, because Moses believed, and so on, this is what each "did." Clearly what they believed was foundational to their actions, activities, and behaviors, but *faith* was realized and displayed in what they *did*! Again, faith is not a synonym for belief. Faith is a synonym for action predicated upon a person's belief.

If one is to consistently exercise and evidence faith, one's beliefs must be informed by one's realization of existential truth. Existential truth is the realization of reliable and trustworthy information that is accepted and affirmed by the individual, which gives direction to how that person lives or should live their life.

If one is to consistently exercise and evidence faith, one's beliefs must be informed by one's realization of existential truth. Existential truth is the information considered to be trustworthy, reliable, and worthy of affirmation and commitment by each individual person and is realized as a result of the unique existence and experiences that make the individual person the person that he or she is and the person that he or she becomes. What one believes, therefore, is predicated upon the sum total of one's unique existence and experiences as one journey through life.

A Clarification Regarding Philippians 4:13

I can do all things through Christ who strengthens me.

(Phil 4:13 NKJV)

This statement by the apostle Paul is often misunderstood. Taken literally, it could suggest that a person can do absolutely anything and everything without limitation. That, however, is not what Paul intended to convey.

Paul was not suggesting that he could do all things that he desired or even imagined. Rather, he was affirming that he could faithfully do all the things that Jesus had called him to say and to do. His confidence was not in unlimited personal ability but in the strength that Christ provided to enable him to fulfill his calling.

In this sense, "all things" refers to all the responsibilities, challenges, and acts of obedience that are required of a person. It speaks to one who seeks to live faithfully before God. It does not refer to every conceivable task or ambition but to those tasks that arise from one's vocation as a servant of Christ.

Paul's life makes this clear. He endured hardship, persecution, hunger, imprisonment, and rejection. Through all of these circumstances, he trusted that Christ would give him the strength necessary to remain faithful, to speak the truth, and to complete the work entrusted to him.

Therefore, this verse should not be understood as a promise of unlimited success but as an affirmation of faithful endurance. It is a declaration that through Christ, one can remain obedient, courageous, and steadfast in doing all that God has truly called one to fulfill.

Distinguishing Between Theology and Religion

Theology is a rational attempt to know and interpret as much about God as one possibly can, especially God's attributes, character, values, purposes, and the relation of God to the universe—including God's relations with human beings.

Additionally, theology is the study of beliefs, rituals, ethics, revelations, symbols, practices, and experiences oriented toward God that human beings consider to be of ultimate and enduring value.

Religion is a commitment to the conclusions that one has reached regarding one's belief's concerning God and contentment regarding the value and meaning of one's relationship with God.

Contrasting Science and Theology

Both science and theology have long served and continue to serve meaningful purposes, and both contribute much to the well-being of humanity with some notable exceptions. One among many exceptions is the scientific development of weapons of mass destruction. Another among many exceptions is the teaching in some religions regarding the offering of human sacrifices (the murder of persons) to appease God.

Science is fundamentally concerned with physics and chemistry and the content and structure of the physical/observable universe. Theology is concerned with the content of humanity's spiritual experiences and concerns including, but not limited to, the meaning and purpose of life, the function of moral freedom, the origin, nature, and function of good and evil, and the anticipated eschatology.

Clearly, science and theology are concerned with two separate and distinct domains, and neither, therefore, should invade each other's space as an authority for both areas of concern.

Regarding Christian Theology

The most important foundation for any reliable Christian theology must be established upon the teaching of Jesus as set forth in the Gospels. There is no doubting that some of Old Testament and New Testament Scriptures as presented in the Bible have much to say that helps to supplement Christian theology, but the teachings of Jesus are the true Christian theological foundation. His teachings, by precept and example as denoted in the Gospels and the connotations derived from it that are consistent with Jesus' teachings, go far in giving to the church and those to whom the Gospel is preached the pathway to the truth about God that all can trust and live with confidence.

Preachers, therefore, are not called to simply read or quote Scripture but to interpret Scripture with a view toward clarifying to the people what the Scriptures call to their attention and why it is still relevant and important for their consideration, their edification, their proclamations, their applications, and their salvation.

If the interpretation of Scripture is flawed, the theology will be flawed. And if the theology is flawed, the interpretation of Scripture will be flawed. The gifts of both one's reasoning ability and the continuing revelations by God to all concerned are essential if the subsequent theological interpretations and proclamations are to be liberated from flaws.

However, the content derived from one's reasoning ability and the continuing revelations one believes to have come from God must, upon reflection, be consistent with and in harmony with what Jesus taught and lived if it is to be properly considered and accepted as solid and reliable Christian theology.

Regarding the "Will" of God

It has been held by many that God's will is multifaceted. That is to say that God's will has several distinct and peculiar features. There are some who would argue that there is only "God's Absolute Will." There are others who suggest that any focus on God's will must also consider God's *Creative* Will, God's *Purposeful* Will, God's *Permissive* Will, and God's *Practical* Will.

When we analyze God's words and actions in the Bible and when we analyze human experiences in the "light" of our theological reflections, it is easy to see why these multifaceted expressions of God's will are justified and necessary in our attempt to try to explain or interpret why God says and does what God says and does. This approach regarding any event, condition, or circumstance can be helpful and should always be considered.

It does no good for anyone to simply say to a mother who has witnessed her young children perish in a house fire that "it was the will of God," as if to leave her with the impression that it was God's will that caused the fire. When there is warfare between nations of the world or between persons where hundreds, thousands, and millions die, and especially under horrifying conditions, it is illogical and misinforming to say, "It was the will of God." What about the person who needs a job and cannot get a job? What about people who are hungry and starving to death? What about nations that are ruled by wicked, dangerous, and intolerant tyrants? What about preachers who take God's name in vain in order to generate fear or psychological control so as to deliberately mislead the people while magnifying and enriching themselves?

Those are some of the situations that require us to make the effort to try to more clearly understand what is and what is not caused by the intentional will of God, and to also try to make some sense of what may be the ultimate reason or function of such occurrences. That can only be done by analyzing each incident, event, or occurrence in the light of the several or more facets or aspects of the will of God.

That being said, suppose our analysis of those various aspects of God's will fails to give us the peace, comfort, and assurance we need concerning God's goodness and God's love for us, as we reflect on our hurt, our shock, our dismay, and disappointment. As difficult as it is to accept, we may at some point in our lives be brought, quite involuntarily, to a place and a point in our thinking where we may be compelled to just surrender to God's permissive will and God's purposeful will, no matter how tragic or hurtful.

It is clearly possible that one or more of these facets of God's will may *seem* to be in conflict with the other facets of God's will, and for this realization, we have no plausible answer other than to encourage those who hurt, grieve, and just can't understand it to put their trust and their hope in God, believing, as the poet once said, that "God moves in a mysterious way His wonders to perform. He plants His footsteps in the sea and He rides upon the storm. Blind unbelief is sure to err and scan God's work in vain, but God is His own interpreter and He will make it plain. His purposes will ripen fast unfolding every hour, the bud may have a bitter taste but sweet will be [the fragrance of] the flower."[2] The fact is, God does what God does, and God will do what God will do, and the *what*, the *why*, the *when*, *where*, and *how* that God provides or allows is beyond our ability to completely understand or explain.

2. William Cowper, "God Moves in a Mysterious Way" (1773).

Regarding Christian Theism

Christian theism is the belief that "God is" and that God is purposefully active in the universe and personally involved in the affairs of persons. Such belief brings people into contact with the mystical, the mysterious, the metaphysical, the moral, and the eschatological. Thus far, these areas of concern and inquiry are above and beyond the tools of science and above and beyond the demonstrable and verifiable "proofs" of persons, no matter what "tools" of inquiry are employed.

The absence of demonstrative and verifiable proofs at the present time does not in any way invalidate the confidence and the assurances that Christian persons derive from many of the beliefs that are affirmed and proclaimed. Christian theists are obligated to maintain certain theories and perspectives about the character and attributes of God and God's designs, purposes, and activities that are reasonable, logical, and worthy of belief and trust.

Some beliefs, perhaps too many beliefs, although well-intended and useful, could be sources of even greater confidence and assurance if affirmed and explained in a more realistic, logical, and coherent way.

To acknowledge Christian theistic limitations in the area of proofs regarding what Christians believe and trust is not inherently fallacious, unreasonable, or heretical. However, the unreasonable, illogical, and manipulative interpretations that many profess to believe are often fallacious, irresponsible, reckless, and quite harmful to the Christian mission and the obligation to soundly preach and teach the gospel of Jesus. The flaws of misinterpretation, misinformation, and disinformation concerning Christian beliefs are flaws that the whole Christian community must endeavor to correct, and preachers must take the lead.

The effort to correct flawed Christian theistic teaching and preaching requires informed demythologizing of the Scriptures where appropriate and necessary in order to unlock the message, its intent, and its meaning, and the same applies to the vast number of metaphors used in the Scriptures. Preachers simply cannot continue preaching myths, metaphors, or clichés as actualities or realities. Properly understood and interpreted, the myths and metaphors in Scripture convey truth and can greatly assist our understanding and our appreciation for the point they are intended to convey through their imagery and symbols. But they are not to be treated as literal actualities in themselves.

The effort to correct flawed teaching and preaching must also compel preachers, especially, to not be lazy, indifferent, or too hurried in preparation to preach and teach or to "jump on the wagon" of whatever is popular at any given time. Preachers who would be helpful and true must take the necessary time to think analytically, to earnestly pray, to follow the evidence where it leads, and to keep their hearts open and receptive to the clarifying input of the Holy Spirit.

Just because much of the content of Christian theistic concerns and cares is mysterious, spiritual, and, at this time, unprovable does not give any preacher license to simply and routinely say anything they please. There has to be some logical, reasonable, and coherent basis in fact and some consistent connection with human experience, past and present, that is undeniably supportive of what preachers, especially, dare to proclaim.

Distinguishing Between Belief and Faith

A *belief* is an assumption or a theory that one holds to be real or true without verifiable facts or proof. Faith is not belief. Faith is not cognitive trust. Faith is not religious or spiritual contemplation. *Faith* is actually living one's life at all times, under all conditions and circumstances, consistently in support of what one claims or professes to believe.

Distinguishing Between Blessed and Bless-ed

The specific and particular pronunciation of the word *blessed* is important because the way that it is spoken or written can convey two different and distinct meanings. It is necessary, therefore, to take great care in how we pronounce it if we are to convey the meaning intended. When we use the word *blessed* in an unhyphenated way, it implies a condition or a circumstance of well-being that has already been realized. When we pronounce the word *bless-ed* in a hyphenated way, it implies not a condition but a function, action, or activity that can enable someone or something to be a blessing and/or enable others to receive or realize blessedness or well-being.

Regarding Myths

Myths are generally looked upon as stories of a particular people or culture regarding the origin and meaning of the universe and what are believed to be the universal experiences of human beings. Myths often utilize an assortment of divine or human characters and literary devices such as metaphor and allegory to affirm and convey a belief or an interpretation regarding why many realizations having to do with the universe and human experience were as they were and are as they are.

Many but not all of the stories in the Bible are myths. To call them myths is not to suggest that they are lies, make-believe, false, or phony, but to suggest that they are other than a scientific attempt to explain something important about the universe and about universal human experience in a descriptive, intelligible, and comprehensible way. To put it another way, myths are a serious attempt to explain or describe certain realizations and experiences by persons in a metaphorical or allegorical way. All myths seem to hint at something in some way deserving of our attention and consideration and should not be summarily or instantly dismissed.

The interpretations and conclusions of science and mathematics today are considered more trustworthy by far than myths, but neither has a lock on absolute truth! A few hundred years from today, many of the "truths" of science and mathematics that we trust and utilize today will either be abandoned or revised in the light of additional experiences and new information.

Even now, "quantum physics" is demonstrating over and over again that the laws of physics that describe physical properties and physical activity in the atomic world or the large-scale physical world cannot and do not apply to smaller physical properties in the subatomic world.

The Doctrine of the Trinity

The doctrine of the Trinity was and is a description of God that was developed by the church "fathers" in the first century after the conclusion of Jesus' active ministry here on earth. There is absolutely nothing in the Gospels or in Jesus' teachings that specifically and clearly proclaims any such doctrine.

Even without this doctrine, it is reasonable and correct to affirm Jesus as the "only begotten" or "one of a kind" Son of God as we consider Jesus' total commitment and devotion to God, the uniqueness of Jesus' mission, the unblemished moral quality of His character, His enduring proclivity toward loving-kindness and forgiveness, and the biblical evidences of His harmonious relationship with God. No other person in history known to us is His equal. Jesus is special, indeed very special. Jesus is one of a kind. However, to fully equate Jesus with God in terms of His "substance," or "is-ness," is a stretch.

One of the reasons Jesus cannot be "identical with God" or "the very God that God is" is because Jesus in His own words affirmed that He died on that cross at Calvary, and *God cannot die*! God has always been, is, and always will be eternal. Consequently, if God had died even for a second (not to even suggest for several days), the entire universe(s) would have died with God, and there would be no record of that.

Additionally, the longest and most detailed mentioning of the Holy Spirit by Jesus in the New Testament occurs in the Gospel of John 14:15–26 and 16:1–15. There is nothing there that equates the Holy Spirit with God as set forth in the doctrine of the Trinity. At best the Holy Spirit seems to be an "agent" of both God and Jesus.

In the Name of the Father, the Son, and the Holy Spirit

This is a formula instituted by the clergy of the early church that has been used for years upon years as a part of most Christian rituals and some prayers. It has a certain familiar historical "ring" to it and such an enduring familiar religious "sound" to it that no one questions what it really means, and the clergy of the church, as far as I know, never did, and do not now, clearly explain what it means.

I offer for consideration and clarification the following perspectives regarding this formula which I believe should be taught and referenced from time to time so as to make it more easily understood and thus more meaningful to those who recite it and to those who hear or read it.

The appropriate use of the formula and any value or meaning derived from the phrase "in the name of," regarding anyone or anything, is strictly dependent upon the context in which it is said and used. It does not have the same specific meaning and function in all situations. It is relative and dependent on the context and the body of all relevant particulars attached to the specific context concerned.

There are some particular instances where "in the name of God" or "in the name of Jesus" contextually implies or declares that what a person has done or what a person is doing or proposes to do is something that is or shall be undertaken and acted upon "as God's representative" or "as the representative of Jesus." For example, when the minister says to a person, "I baptize you in the name of the Father and in the name of the Son," it should be taught and properly understood to mean this: "As the representative of God and as the representative of Jesus, I baptize you."

In certain particular rituals and ceremonies such as consecrations, ordinations, marriages, funerals, dedications, and so on, it is appropriate to utilize the formula. However that formula does not have the same meaning when cited or referenced in all rituals, ceremonies, or prayers and should not be routinely included or expressed because of necessary differentiation and because in many instances "in the name of God" or "in the name of Jesus" is not cited by the minister as a representative of God or Jesus, but to indicate that the minister or the person praying or officiating is doing so with "trust and confidence" in the ability of God and Jesus to respond consistent with their love for us, their goodwill toward us, and the righteousness of their character.

There are times when "in the name of God" is best understood to mean a "servant of God" or "in accordance with the will of God" or "under the auspices of God" or "under the protection of God," and so on. Likewise, "in the name of Jesus" may mean "as a follower of my Leader, Jesus" or "at the instruction of Jesus" or "as a witness for Jesus" or "in support of the purposes of Jesus."

Again, the context must always be considered, as it will be determinant. Correct and intelligible usage depend upon the *specific context* in which the formula is being employed.

There is a song entitled, "In the Name of Jesus" that is sung by a church each and every time the congregation assembles for worship. The use of that song in that context is not intended to address the members of that church particularly as *representatives* of Jesus but as *followers* of Jesus and as students (disciples) of Jesus who desire to learn more about Jesus and to become more like Jesus—students who seek the wisdom, the guidance, the inspiration, and the motivation of Jesus among other expectations, concerns, and cares.

The main point being made in this analysis is that the formula or phrase "in the name of the Father, Son, and Holy Spirit" is not a one-size-fits-all formula, and it cannot be properly understood or employed to convey deep meaning to the people when it is used as a general routine formula or expression without consideration of the context. It cannot be stressed enough that usage of the formula must consider the specific context in which one proposes to use it, and clarification regarding how it is being used *must be offered* to the people from time to time if they are to understand it and if it is to be meaningful to them.

Addendum: Two Additional Points to Consider

"In the name of the Holy Spirit" seems to be quite different from the other components of the formula as its function is guidance, instruction, edification, and inspiration. A reference to the Holy Spirit in rituals and ceremonies, therefore, requires greater consideration of the context and greater consideration of what is precisely meant.

When we recite the formula including "in the name of the Holy Spirit," we are not implying or suggesting that we are representatives of the Holy Spirit but that we and the people have the opportunity to be the beneficiaries of the finished works (purpose and function) of the Holy Spirit.

So, when we say "in the name of the Holy Spirit," it seems to be a way of saying to people, "May we be informed and enlightened by the Holy Spirit," or "May we be guided and edified"—or "inspired and strengthened," and so on—"by the Holy Spirit."

The expression "for the sake of Jesus," or "for Jesus' sake," means "in the interest/support of Jesus' purposes, mission, and concerns and in the interest of saying and doing whatever we can to affirm and uphold all that Jesus is, all that Jesus stands for, and all that Jesus means."

While the expression "for the sake of Jesus" is most appropriate usage, the expression "for Jesus' namesake" is not. It is a misnomer that obfuscates.

Regarding Salvation

To the average layperson and to many preachers, salvation is the assured entrance of a person into heaven and the avoidance of everlasting punishment and suffering in hell. I cannot affirm that perspective as upheld and proclaimed in that way.

I do affirm that salvation is the realization of eternal peace and harmony with God that is freely and lovingly offered to us as a result of God's love and the love of Jesus for us. In the interest of our eternal well-being, Jesus lived His righteous and self-sacrificing life as a love offering to God on our behalf.

God, being so pleased with the purposes and the quality of Jesus' entire life, has been moved to put into full force and effect an opportunity for all persons to be saved. It is through Jesus that persons who accept the opportunity are rescued from everlasting isolation and estrangement from God and consequently are reconciled with God forever.

SECTION II

THE PERSON AND WORK OF JESUS

Regarding Jesus as Preacher and Teacher

Contrary to what some and perhaps many may think, Jesus was not a simplistic or elementary preacher and teacher. Jesus was a deeply thoughtful and analytical theologian and a competent moral philosopher who expressed His revealing and meaningful views and teachings in the common language of the people. His proclamations and instructions, however, were comprehensive, profound, meaningful, useful, and practical (action oriented) as opposed to untenable theoretical speculation, hyperbole, and foolish rhetorical content.

Regarding Jesus as Redeemer

How and why Jesus' mission and salvific purpose here on earth was ever characterized as a "redemptive mission" has been troubling many for years. To describe His mission as a redemptive mission is akin to describing it as a "commercial transaction" rather than a loving realization and interaction between God and Jesus that provides the path for persons to be reconciled with God.

The meaning of *redemption* implies that something was bought or purchased by someone in return for something, and that surely seems to be more akin to a commercial or business transaction concerning a commodity rather than the great realization of love and manifestation of love that inspired and undergirded Jesus' salvific mission. The very concept of *redemption*, therefore, sends the wrong message.

Jesus did not "purchase" anyone from the consequences of sin, or "purchase" a way for persons to realize eternal favor and harmony with God. Jesus lovingly, earnestly, and faithfully *gave all of Himself* toward that end. To say that Jesus gave all of Himself toward that end means that Jesus' *spirit, heart, mind, body, feelings*, and also His *teachings* and *practices* were all lovingly, faithfully, and consistently focused upon and directed toward eternal *reconciliation* (eternal peace and harmony) between God and all persons.

That was not a "deal." That was not a "transaction." That was not a "commercial operation." That was and is the realization and manifestation of divine love, concern, and care for all persons at its ultimate and most meaningful level. Jesus did not "buy" God's love, forgiveness, and mercy for us. Jesus' love for God and humanity and God's love for Jesus and humanity are the dynamics that make possible our liberation from the consequences of *sin* and its symptoms, while providing for the realization of our eternal reconciliation with God.

Jesus Alone, Jesus Only: "The Leader of the Church"

Historically, during Jesus' ministry here on earth, His disciples usually referred to Jesus as Lord or Master. The title *Master* was seldom, if ever, used by the early church after the crucifixion and resurrection of Jesus. Almost two thousand years ago, therefore, the church began referring to Jesus or addressing Jesus by several different titles, such as *Christ*, *Lord*, *Savior*, *Redeemer*, and *Son of God*. The church has continuously taught and indoctrinated Christians and would-be Christians to use those same titles when referencing or addressing Jesus across the years to this day.

It is my view that Jesus *is* and must always be referenced and addressed as our Savior and as the only begotten (one of a kind) Son of God. Along with the employment of those two titles, however, I consider it to be of utmost importance that Christians (the church) begin referring to Jesus and addressing Jesus more frequently both privately and publicly in our sermons, speeches, prayers, and testimonies as "our Leader," and this should be done in a deliberate, continual, and emphatic way.

I earnestly believe this can be the starting point towards the healing of so many divisions throughout the various expressions of the church and that it would enable all believers or "could-be believers" to experience a constant and reinforcing reminder that Jesus is not only the Savior and the Lord and worthy to be worshiped and praised, but also the *Leader* of His church. Jesus is not the Leader in a mysterious and nebulous way but in a clearly understood and practical way.

Jesus is the Leader of the church and must be affirmed and followed if the church is to be fully concretized, fully realized, and faithful and true. Unity and harmony under His leadership must be and *always* be among the highest goals and aspirations of the church if the church is to actually *be* the church. This will not be achieved all at once. It will take time, but it must be done, and it can be done. Acknowledging and faithfully following Jesus as the Leader of the church is the necessary starting point, and the church must teach it and live it with great and unrelenting energy and emphasis from now onward.

Clergy-persons are not the leaders of the church. For the sake of order, continuity, and the processing of clearly defined and necessary procedures and in the interest of unity and harmony, particular clergy-persons are set apart and authorized to safeguard and manage the affairs of the church. But, again, clergy-persons are not the leaders of the church; they are particular Servants; they are the Heralds, the Kerygmatics, the Caregivers, and the Counselors of Jesus to the church—to all persons who earnestly seek and strive to follow Jesus, and to the entire family of humanity.

Surely, there have always been, and there still are, some egomaniacal charismatic personalities in and throughout the church who project themselves as leaders of the church and who, because of their popularity and cleverness, deceive themselves and many into believing that they are the leaders or among the leaders of the church. However, no one and absolutely no one but Jesus *is our Leader*! Jesus is the Leader of the entire body of the Christian Community which is the church. His teachings and "their meanings" properly understood are His instructions to the church. His purposes, values, concerns, and cares must be or become the priorities of the church and worthy of the acceptance and the affirmation of all humanity. It is the mission of the church to say and do all that it can to communicate the gospel persuasively to all humanity.

The gospel is the "good news." It is the trustworthy information and the vital information that Jesus taught and lived, and it gives to humanity its best opportunity to be reconciled with God and its best opportunity to help facilitate peace and harmony throughout the family of humanity.

If the church is to be faithful, persuasive, effective, and productive regarding its mission in the name of Jesus to the world, the church must first get its own house in order and become better positioned to preach, teach, and live the gospel. To be sure, the church that we observe today is represented as various denominations, associations, and "independent" churches. These continuing divided, disharmonious, and dysfunctional expressions and representations of the church regarding all doctrines, beliefs, and priorities must be healed. Many of these denominations, associations, and independent churches, in fact, are often competitive and too inwardly and selfishly focused. Many persons in this world clearly realize this, can make no sense of it, and refuse to be a part of it.

The status quo must be healed, but it cannot be healed until the church firmly acknowledges Jesus as the Leader and commits to Him, His teachings, and their "meaning," which extends beyond mere quotations. For as long as "the church" is seen and experienced by so many persons as a confused, divided, and fragmented institution or body of "believers," it will be flawed and will seriously be hindered or even denied the opportunity to faithfully pursue and realize the goal, the mission, and service to all of humanity as prescribed by Jesus.

The "Christian church" should also reject any and all references or descriptions of itself as a "faith community" or "community of faith." There are many of us who say that we are Christians. If indeed we are Christians, we are not merely a community of faith. We are *the church* and *Jesus is our Leader*—not Abraham, Moses, David, or any of the prophets, and not Peter or Paul or any clergy-persons past, present, or future, no matter what their title. Jesus alone is the *Leader* of the church. *Jesus only* is *our Leader*!

Jesus, the Embodiment of God's Grace

Jesus made no references to *grace* anywhere in the Gospels because the word *grace* had not yet been created/invented or set forth in the languages of Jesus' day to the extent that Paul did. Paul did not specifically teach that Jesus is the embodiment and the personification of grace, but I do. Although Jesus did not use the word *grace*, it seems clear to me that Jesus understood Himself to be the supreme embodiment (the manifestation and personification) of what Paul was expressing when Paul taught the importance and the efficacy of *grace* to and for all humanity.

Paul, in several instances, implied but did not directly or specifically teach that Jesus was the embodiment and personification of God's grace, but I do and I shall. Jesus as the embodiment of "grace" is the one who offers to all persons the opportunity to be saved. Through Him and for His sake, God provides to humanity the opportunity for reconciliation and eternal peace and harmony with God, which is what salvation means.

Whatever Jesus said and did, whatever Jesus affirms and upholds in the interest of our well-being here on earth and throughout all eternity, is "grace." Grace is not just a word, it is *the word* that represents and makes intelligible the special provision—the special gift that springs forth from the heart of God and the love of God to help us in our helplessness and in our despair—and Jesus is the embodiment, the personification, and manifestation of it in all its indications and ramifications.

Whenever Jesus spoke about God's love for us and His love for us, He was speaking about grace. Whenever He made a promise or commitment to us, He was speaking of Himself as the embodiment of God's grace. All His words and actions were, in essence, manifestations of God's grace, which is the "help," the "intervention," the "assurance," and the "instruction" that we need in our weakness, our uncertainty, and our helplessness.

Jesus as the embodiment (personification and manifestation) of "God's grace" can be seen and heard in His own words when we substitute the word *grace*. For example:

- "I have come that you might have life" = "*Grace* has come to you through Me so that you might have life."
- "Come unto Me and I, *the embodiment of God's grace*, will give you confidence and peace within."
- "I am the way, the truth, . . ." etc. = "I am *the embodiment of the grace of God* who will give to you all you need to know and to practice in order to be pleasing and acceptable to God forever."
- Had Jesus utilized the word *grace*, He would have said in John 3:16, "God so loved all humanity that He made of Me and is using Me as the one and only person who fully embodies and personifies *God's grace*, and anyone who believes in Me [i.e., anyone who accepts, trusts, and depends on the "grace" that I am] will discover that to do so will provide the sustaining power that will strengthen their effort to live up to the expectations of God, to persevere in good and noble endeavor, to witness for God and Me in honest and trustworthy preaching, teaching, and serving in My name and for My sake, and so on, and shall not fail because *grace*, the grace that I am, will give all such persons confidence that they are secure and that they will be OK."

Jesus, in fact, says to humanity, "The *grace* that I am will empower and enable all persons who welcome and accept Me to prevail over doubts and fears, the persistence of evil, and the impacts of rejection and disappointments, and so on, which they presently encounter and will continue to encounter as they journey through this life."

In essence, had Jesus directly utilized the word *grace* (which was not a part of His vocabulary) in His self-references, He would have said "*Grace*, the grace that *I am*, will assure and give, to any and all persons who welcome and accept Me, the aid, the hope, and the confidence needed to persevere all the way to the end of this life's journey and to the end of their mission in My name. And when they come to the end of their journey and their mission, *I*, the one and only embodiment and personification of God's *grace*, will provide for each and all the realization of a quality of life with God that shall have no end."

While it is true that the ancient Hebrews and their descendants used a few specific words that referenced grace as God's protection, favor, mercy, and so on, it is to be noted that such usage was limited to some particular Hebrew person or persons and, of course, themselves as a people. So, there was no universal application that extended beyond the Hebrew people. Jesus as the embodiment of God's grace is the precious and unique gift from God offered universally to and available to *all* humanity

I Am the Way, the Truth, and the Life

On one occasion, Jesus defined and described Himself in this manner:

I am the way.

This is Jesus' way of saying, "I am the road, I am the path, I am the map, and I am the guide; I am the resource that provides for you your best opportunity and the means to acquire enduring well-being and to become all that you have been created to be."

I am the truth.

"In Me you will find and you can receive [internalize] and utilize the most reliable information you can possibly have and need to have regarding your proper sense of direction, your proper relationship with God, and your proper relationship with other persons."

I am the life.

"I am your empowerment. I am the 'wellspring' and the 'content' of your spiritual life, your moral life, and the qualitative life that generates within you the capacity you need for the realization of eternal life, which is eternal harmony and fellowship with God."

No person shall come to the father except through Me.

"I am, therefore, the means specifically offered to you through which you can 'experience' harmony and proper relationship with God and with other persons and be privileged to continue your journey consciously, self-consciously, and conscientiously as a meaningful participant in the eternal purposes of God."

I Am the Life

When Jesus declares, "I am the life," He is declaring the following:

"I am the source of your transformation."

"I am the source of the life that you are being taught to live."

"I am the source of the life that you are expected to live."

"I am the resource that facilitates your transition into a quality of life that is eternal."

Abide in Me

"Abide in Me" is Jesus' way of saying, "Think of Me often. Fully receive into your consciousness and into your being who I am and how deeply and sincerely I love you. Meditate and reflect often on all that I have taught you, what I have revealed to you, what I have done for you, and what I have promised you."

Whose Disciple Are You?

This is a question that each person should seriously consider and answer with genuine confidence and commitment. Discipleship has to do with the relationship between a single master, visionary, teacher, leader, exemplar, and guide and their followers, learners, advocates, and servants.

I have admiration, respect, and appreciation for many persons. However, I am not a disciple of Abraham, Isaac, Jacob, Moses, David, or any prophet nor any person other than Jesus.

SECTION III

THE HUMAN CONDITION AND SPIRITUAL FORMATION

III.A — The Moral Struggle and Human Brokenness

Regarding Obedience and Goodness

In most religions, obedience to certain laws, rules, and prescriptions, including what are represented as God's laws, rules, and prescriptions, dominate practically everything having to do with that religion. If one would be a "good" person and a "good" practitioner of that religion, obedience to the laws, rules, and prescriptions is absolutely required. It is clearly understood, however, that while obedience to laws, rules, and prescriptions can provide for "orderly conduct" and "directed conduct," blind or coerced obedience to laws, rules, and prescriptions alone cannot transform a person into the self-motivated way of thinking, feeling, and behaving indicative of the character and the attributes of a "good person."

At best, obedience that is consistent with what one is ordered to do, required to do, or forced to do is done in the interest of receiving a reward or the avoidance of punishment. That is compliance, but compliance is not goodness, and forced compliance is not goodness.

Compliance is dictated and controlled behavior. *Goodness* is a positive and beneficial way of thinking, behaving, and living that is the result of a willful and freely embraced commitment to the values that give a person and all of humanity the best opportunity to evidence and genuinely practice such values as kindness, justice, goodwill, forgiveness, empathy, compassion, and so on. There are other supportive values to be sure, and the thing they all have in common is that they operate towards the well-being of God, one's self, and the well-being of all other persons.

Goodness, like love, is a realization. It cannot be imposed upon a person or forced into a person's self/being; it is the voluntary affirmation and commitment to the values we believe to be inspired by God that best facilitate and sustain peaceful and harmonious interactions and relationships between ourselves and all persons, including God.

Goodness is an ideal, but it does not become real until it is freely and willfully embraced and acted upon by persons to the extent that goodness becomes consistently manifested through their attitudes and behaviors in all actions, activities, and processes that favorably impact others in ways that are beneficent, respectful, and kind.

Regarding Human Sinfulness

Sin is not an act or a particular thing that one does. Sin is a *condition*, a "sickness of the self" that has to do with a willful and self-generated distortion of the self that allows the self to be comfortable and satisfied with alienation from God and thus in a state of disharmony with God and consequently in disharmony with other persons.

Sin becomes, therefore, a way of life that is governed by a perspective regarding ourselves that distorts our self-understanding to the extent that we are prevented from realizing our proper relationship with God, which should be our highest aim and our ultimate goal.

The emergence of the sinful condition in us has much to do with what we in error value and what we in error believe, because what we value and what we believe will become our priority, our preoccupation, and our proclivity regarding the way of life that we choose to live.

The acts that we do and the activities we engage in that we call sins are better viewed and described as symptoms of sin. They are symptoms of the "sickness of the self." This sickness of the self is driven by the self's willful submission to the spirit of megalomania (delusions of personal grandeur) and by the will to be powerful in order to satisfy, uphold, and defend one's megalomania.

When megalomania is allowed to persist unhealed, it will catapult the self into rebellion against God and into rivalry or competition with God. Sin becomes more and more evident as the self rejects the positive values that God affirms as "the good" in favor of those negative values that support and strengthen the continuation of the sickness within—the megalomania.

"The good" is that which serves the well-being of all. Well-being has to do with freedom from a distorted perspective regarding one's self and a distorted perspective regarding God and other selves (persons). Well-being also means to have the full realization of the best opportunity to become the self that God intended and still intends for the self to be: loving, kind, just and fair, compassionate, caring, self-giving, forgiving, respectful of others, and so on. But that can only be realized subsequent to one's authentic loving and respectful relationship with God and one's sincere affirmation of God as the subject and the object of one's utmost service and devotion.

Regarding the Fig Leaves of Adam and Eve

After Adam and Eve (the first man and woman), blatantly operated contrary to the instruction and the expectations of God, they became aware of their sinful condition and thus experienced a profound sense of guilt, inadequacy, and the loss of their sense of innocence, which caused them to feel naked or shamefully "exposed" to the scrutiny and the critical judgment of God.

They did not know anything about theology, psychology, or psychiatry; therefore, the physical covering of much of their bodies with *something* was their feeble attempt to hide, to alter, to conceal, or to camouflage what they did not want God to know. This, they hoped, would shield them from the disappointment and critical judgment of God and, thereby, mitigate or lessen their sense of guilt and the loss of their sense of innocence. In other words, they were "putting up a front" they thought could enable them and their sinful action and behavior to be, preferably, unexposed—or at least to be less exposed.

Clearly, they believed that a successful "cover-up" distorting or limiting their exposure to the critical scrutiny and judgment of God would operate to relieve their sense of guilt and restore to them the comfort and peace of a "sense" of innocence, even if not the return of their actual innocence *in fact*. All cover-ups are intended to conceal, to pretend, and to deflect.

Some of our modern day "fig leaves" are many and varied. Among them are arrogance, hypocrisy, denial, deceit, distortion, plastic surgery, and some mind-altering drugs.

Is a Clean Slate Possible?

There are many persons who believe, preach, and teach that Jesus Christ and God can, as they say, wipe the slate (of a person's life) clean no matter how unclean, dirty, shameful, or awful it may be.

Jesus did not teach that. Jesus taught that God is inclined to be forgiving and merciful but said nothing about God wiping anyone's slate clean or giving anyone a "clean slate." The fact is, our history—i.e., our actions, attitudes, behaviors, choices, and decisions—cannot be "dehistorized" or "unhistorized." Just as a person who has been murdered cannot be restored to a state in which the murder never occurred, the one who committed the act cannot undo its historical reality. The murderer can be forgiven, and the penalty for the murder can be set aside (which is what *mercy* is), but the action—the historical fact that a murder occurred and was committed by a particular person, in a particular way, at a particular time—cannot be erased or undone.

If the expression "God wipes the slate clean" is a suggestion that God treats some things as if they did not happen, that *does not mean that what happened did not happen* or is made to disappear as a fact or event in history; it is only representative of God's prerogative to forgive what happened and to be merciful regarding any penalty, if God should so decide. No, the slate cannot "be wiped clean"—the many choices, decisions, actions, and behaviors that are a person's history cannot be undone. Thank God for forgiveness and grace!

Regarding Forgiveness

Forgiveness is not a feeling. It is a decision. Forgiveness, when utilized, is an important resource in the dynamics having to do with human relations. The forgiveness of an offender is not a panacea for broken and damaged relations between the offender and the offended party. In order to understand the meaning and function of forgiveness, one should first consider that forgiveness is an act of the will and not an emotion or feeling.

Unlike love, forgiveness is not a spontaneous realization that happens independent of one's "will." Forgiveness is a choice. It is a decision that is deliberately made and implemented. The decision to forgive does not heal the hurt caused by the offender, and it does not undo the estrangement or brokenness in relations between the offender and the offended person. Additionally, the objectionable words, actions, and behaviors of the offender are not banished from the mind of the offended party just because the decision has been made to forgive the offender.

Forgiveness is like the "pause" button on a remote or audio/video device. When one forgives, it puts the entire matter in a "paused position" and provides for the offended party the opportunity to mitigate or disable their thoughts and feelings that are negative and hostile. If the offended party does not utilize the opportunity thoughtfully and wisely with a view toward neutralizing the hurtful words, actions, and behaviors generated by the offender, malice, hatred, and the passion for revenge will ensue. That is problematic and even dangerous because hatred, in particular, can only be satisfied by knowledge of the suffering or the destruction of the offender.

Therefore, forgiveness is a "first step" decision that provides the offended party with the opportunity to process alternative thoughts and feelings other than malice, hatred, and revenge. One such possibility that occurs as a result of this process is the opportunity for reconciliation. However, if reconciliation is to occur, a "second step" must be taken by the offender, and that is for the offender to send a clear signal in some discernible way to the offended party that reconciliation is desirable.

A "third step" then becomes necessary to fully realize reconciliation, and it has to with repentance either spoken or demonstrated by the offender to the offended party in some clearly understood way.

Forgiveness is only the first step in this process, but it is probably the most important step because if it is not taken, the second step and third step will have little chance of emerging.

III.B — The Self: Identity, Consciousness, and Inner Life

Regarding the Heart

The Bible often refers to "the heart." Jesus did likewise. In our everyday discourse, we also make references to the heart; but in all these instances, references to the heart have nothing to do with the biological muscle and organ in our bodies that pumps oxygenated blood to the cells. So, if loving someone or caring for someone or doing something with all our heart has nothing to do with the biological muscle/organ in our bodies, what are we talking about when we refer to the heart?

The heart is a synergistic realization, a synergic manifestation. Synergism is a process where two or more unlike and distinct things combine to form yet another thing that is totally different from the two individual, unlike, and distinct things that formed it. Water, for example, is the realization and manifestation that emerges from the synergistic interaction of hydrogen and oxygen.

From my view, the heart is a particular and unique "realized entity" that emerges from the synergistic relationship of a person's thoughts and feelings. The "heart," therefore, is a perspective, a passion, and a proclivity that is generated within one's self by the synergistic (i.e., the interactive and collaborative) thoughts and feelings of the particular "self" concerned.

Regarding the "Soul-Self"

Theologically, from my view, the words *soul* and *self* are equivalent and interchangeable. Both are references to the spiritual and nonmaterial entity that allows or provides for the realization and manifestation of the separate, unique, and distinct personhood of each human being. Each soul-self is

God's gift to soul-self It is a gift that allows us to "be" and to "become." It provides for each of us the opportunity to develop our individual and personal essence in this universe, which is also called the world.

Who we are and who we become, with reference to ourselves as "persons," is the result of the creative dynamics of our existence, our experiences, our beliefs, our choices, our decisions, and our actions. We are and we become, therefore, the content of our "history," which is inclusive of every moment that we exist and live in this universe.

We are not our names; our names are simply what we are called. We are not the physical features of the bodies with which we are associated. *We are our history.* Our history, therefore, becomes the "essence" of our soul-self as it is the "stuff" that makes us who we are—the source of our specific and unique personhood.

We cannot delete our history. We can only add to it for as long as we exist and live in this universe. Our failure at some point in time to be able to remember or recall all or parts of our history is not a deletion of it; it only detaches a person from the memory of it. The actual content of our history cannot be deleted or destroyed. When we, as persons, survive the transition process from time into eternity, our history, the essence of our soul-self and the source of our personhood will remain a stable and enduring reality forever.

There is no time in eternity: no past and no future. In eternity, even the concepts of past and future by persons other than God is not possible. Eternity is a perpetual state of "is-ness" and "wholeness." It is a constant and continual present—an eternal *now* where one has no sense of beginnings and endings, no yesterdays, and no tomorrows, only the constant perpetual here and now.

If we try hard enough, we can recall occasional, limited, or brief experiences of such realizations. Even here in this universe, we have all had moments when we experienced joy and bliss and meaning and purpose that seemed to transcend time and any thoughts about past and future and beginnings and endings—that is, until the concept of time intruded upon our thoughts. Everything in that special moment of realization was wonderful until we "snapped out of it," as it were, and connected our experience with the realization of the boundaries, the limitations, of time. It was then and there that time or the concept of time operated adversely to our sense of the joy and the well-being we had derived from that momentary realization of is-ness, nowness, wholeness, and completeness. Time will not impact us in that way in eternity because in eternity there is no time and no concept of time by any person.

Time "in eternity" is an oxymoron and simply cannot be. With God being the one exception, even the concept of time cannot be formed in eternity, and if it were even remotely possible, that so-called eternity would be precluded from being the eternity that concerns us.

Regarding the Loss of One's Soul

Jesus asked the question, "What does it profit a person to gain the whole world and lose their soul?" (see Matt 16:26).

Regarding this inquiry, it is so unfortunate that many preachers and others deduced that Jesus was speaking with reference to the eschatology and the final consequence of persons who make the acquisition of fame, fortune, material things, and "power" their greatest goal and the essence of their life. Jesus, however, was not suggesting in His caveat that such persons would be condemned to hell by God in the "judgment." From my perspective, that seems not to be the case.

Jesus was suggesting such persons, even in this life, would ultimately lose "self"-respect and their appreciation for the proper realizations of the deeper and true meaning of the purpose and value of their "self," and lose the opportunities (or not make use of the opportunities) granted by God for their self to become what the self is intended to be, which is a reflection and representation of the image and likeness of God in this world.

Regarding the Location of My "Self" Before Its Association with My Body

Any concerns or curiosities we may have regarding the location of the "self" before its bodily association is predicated upon the assumption that the self had to be somewhere other than "to be" or "to become."

I have tried to make it abundantly clear that *it is not possible* to apply or compare specific quantifications, descriptions, and measurements in and of this universe when trying to comprehend eternity and eternal conditions and operations.

We simply must, therefore, resist the notion or the tendency to view the self as a quantity of substance that can be measured or located, because the self has no physical properties. Consequently, asking the question "Where was the 'self' before its association with the body?" is not the relevant or appropriate question. The most relevant and appropriate question is "What or where is the 'origin' of the self?"

I respond, therefore, in this way. The self is clearly a unique expression of one's opportunity "to be" and "to become" a nonmaterial and infinite entity fully capable of realizing consciousness and self-consciousness.

Each and every self was formed and is still being formed in the creative vision and will of God, the Generator and the Concertizer who brings forth from the realm of possibility all that is made "real" or allowed to become "real."

The "creative vision of God" and the "creative will of God" are not "places" (in the sense that we use that word). They are "processes" and, therefore, cannot be viewed as locations where the specific position of anything can be determined or located. Yet, the origin and realization of the self have become, thus far, a progressive result of those processes with more development and realizations to come. The self therefore can only be correctly and properly viewed as a "unique and creative expression" of the vision and the will of God that began with God and is still part of the processes of God enabling it "to be" and "to become" more than it ever was and presently is.

Lastly, it is appropriate to analyze and evaluate the self as a "quality of being" but never as a "quantity of being" that submits to quantifications or measurements that are relevant only to our definitions, usages, and descriptions of the physical universe.

Like our experience of the reality and the presence of the self, we experience the reality and the presence of such unique entities and "things in themselves," such as love, happiness, peace, anger, hatred, power, heartache, and sadness. It is somewhat ludicrous to even ask, "Where was love before

I realized or experienced it? Or peace, or heartache, or happiness, or grief? And where did they go when they departed from me or I was no longer aware of their presence or activity within or upon me?"

We can surely experience and describe the impact and the effect of love, peace, anger, suspicion, trust; but we cannot express what they are or where they reside quantitatively. We have no objective reference point that allows or permits us to even conceive a location where they come from, where they reside, or where they go beyond our experience with their presence. We only have the experience and realization of their reality, their presence, and their effect.

The Principle of Uncertainty

The historic concept of the "principle of uncertainty" is a unique and well-defined feature of quantum physics, which in part has to do with the random variations and probabilities that impact physics at the subatomic level.

There is, however, the "principle of uncertainty" that is manifest in all areas of human experience and all of nature also. It is clear to me, and should be clear to all persons, that God has provided for the operations of the principle of uncertainty regarding many actions and events in the universe and regarding many of the events, conditions, experiences, and outcomes that uniquely impact all persons and all expressions of nature that we call natural forces and processes.

This is consistent with and the result of God's decision to limit His own freedom in order to grant some freedom to all components of creation, including the "free will" that God grants to each person.

This gift of freedom in large measure and in so many ways was deemed by God to be necessary in order to counteract the certainty of monotony and boredom that would be realized without the operation of the principle of uncertainty. Uncertainty as we experience it is, in some way, a consequence of the realty of freedom—"real" and "true" freedom—in and throughout all components and expressions of the universe.

As we journey through this life and this present universe/world for the few years we spend here, *it is not certainty but uncertainty* that keeps us alert, that keeps us challenged, that keeps us reflecting, projecting, thinking, planning, hoping, and striving. It is not certainty but uncertainty that often instructs us to be reasonably careful and cautious and not to take anything for granted. It is uncertainty that rescues us from the dread and discomfort of monotony and boredom. The principle of uncertainty prevents us from knowing in advance the full implications and outcomes of all our thoughts, decisions, and actions for some of the reasons I have set forth and, in a mysterious but unique way, helps to make life more interesting.

The millions of people who patronize basketball, baseball, and football games, for example, would soon stop watching or attending any games if they knew with absolute certainty the outcome of every game in advance. It would not take long for the patrons of those games to become disturbingly bored. The same is true for those who have fun gambling. If a person gambled every day and won a prize every time he or she gambled, it would not take long for that to become boring also. The fascination and enchantment of gambling connects their uncertainty with their hopes in a peculiar way that challenges and excites them.

God limits His own freedom to know in advance the outcome of all things for similar reasons and more. Can you truly imagine God—who is, has been, and will be *forever*—knowing "in advance" the outcome of all things?

That would be the full equivalent of God watching the same movie over and over and over and over *forever*, and that would be extremely monotonous, boring, and intolerable, even to God.

Another thing, not only does God limit His freedom to know all things. Of course, God *can* know all things but chooses not to. God also restrains Himself from doing all that He could do in order to uphold the operations of freedom and the principle of uncertainty in this world and in this universe.

God does maintain the freedom, the right, and the ability to act and to intervene in all things and all matters whenever and wherever He chooses or decides, but God is not inclined to abort or eradicate His decisions regarding many of the operations of freedom and the principle of uncertainty in our experiences and in the universe.

III.C — The Body, Suffering, and Adversity

Regarding the Body

The human body is not the "self." It is a material and physiological apparatus that accompanies the self in this universe and is the instrument through which the self becomes manifested and experienced by other "selves" in this universe. Our earliest realization and awareness of our "self" was not physical. We had an awareness of our self before we knew we were associated with a body. There are also moments in time, even now, when we are oblivious concerning the body with which we are associated but still experience our awareness of our self without any reference to a physical image or consciousness of the body or any body parts.

Practically all the activity of the body is sensory or sense oriented. The activity and the experience of the self is spiritual. When the body is biologically active and functioning, it can feel physical pleasure and pain, but it cannot independently know, realize, or appropriate the value and meaning of love, happiness, truth, sorrow, fellowship, and so on. It is the self alone that experiences love, happiness, truth, sorrow, and fellowship. Although these kinds of realizations may impact or affect the body in some way, the impact or effect that is observed in or on the body under such conditions is a physical or chemical symptom (appearance) made manifest by the spiritual realizations of the self, and is not simply a condition or impact that is sourced by physical or physiological stimuli.

The body can directly and immediately connect with physical or chemical stimuli such as pain, hunger, thirst, exhaustion, sexual gratification, sweet flavors, and pleasant aromas, but the body cannot directly experience the evidences of spiritual content and appropriate its impact, value, or meaning in the same way or with the same discernment as does the self.

All spiritual activity and all spiritual value and meaning must first become realized by the self and then possibly made evident in some symptoms that may be detectable in or on the body in a physical or physiological way. The primary or fundamental impelling force of the spiritual, however, is not sensory or physiological but the result of the unique realizing and discerning abilities and capabilities of the self.

It should be clear that the feelings and the condition of the body and the emotions and condition of the self are not the same. Even the impact of the passage of time impacts the body and the self differently. The death and destruction of the body will certainly be realized by the self. But the self which is a spiritual and eternal being will be liberated from its association with its' body and will maintain its vitality forever.

It is acknowledged that there is a relationship between the body and the self. But the true short-term and limited purpose and function of the body in this world (universe) is to provide the self with a practical means to navigate the physical/material universe, including time and space, and to reveal and make known to other selves the presence of the self that is associated with a particular body.

Regarding the Body (Additionally)

I am certain—positively certain—that all persons experienced a self-consciousness of being alive even before they connected their "aliveness" or their self-consciousness with a particular accompanying body.

The inability to recall that consciousness and self-consciousness with specific reference points in time is not unusual and does not matter. At that stage of being, your mother fed the body, changed diapers on the body, and responded to cries emanating from the body. Your inability to recall it at that stage in your life or at any time since those occurrences makes no difference. It happened. You had no vocabulary or symbols to express it or to enter that realization into your memory bank, but it happened.

Moreover, there are times even now when we become so lost in our thoughts that our bodies become oblivious to our "self." That is what primarily happens when we are driving and texting or sometimes daydreaming or just listening to music.

It is not the awareness or references to our bodies that gives to us a true, consistent, and enduring sense of our "self." The self is always self-conscious of its being in its own unique way. Even if you were to undergo full-body plastic surgery or experience a complete change in the appearance and features of your body, as the result of a fire or other accident, you would retain a continuous and consistent sense of "I am."

Consciousness of being alive, or being a living self, transcends any awareness we have or may have concerning the body with which our self is associated.

Regarding Pain and Adversity

Pain and adversity are two of the most distinguished but undocumented "instructors" that any person will ever have. Pain and adversity have no diplomas or degrees, and they are not certified by any human government, commission, association, or agency, but they are among the best qualified, informative, and effective teachers in the classroom of human existence.

If we are able to avoid the onset of Alzheimer's and dementia as we journey through life, it is not likely we will ever forget the many lessons we learn about ourselves, others, and life itself from the tutelage of pain and adversity.

In the classroom of human existence, pain and adversity never politely ask anyone, "May I have your attention?" When they arrive or appear in our lives, they immediately get our attention and maintain it until their peculiar course of study and reflection is completed.

The deep meaning and value of the lessons learned do not reside in the information and the instruction we gain but in the application and the utilization of it as we continue our journey in the universe.

Regarding Redemption and Redemptive Suffering

Redemption literally means "to buy something back." More specifically, it means to buy something back that is under the control or the prerogative of someone else.

I cannot accept the doctrine of redemption as a valid description or explanation of what Jesus Christ has done for the salvation of all humanity. Redemption denotes a commercial transaction where something is bought and something is sold. God did not sell our salvation; God did not and does not sell forgiveness and mercy to Jesus, and Jesus did not purchase it. Our salvation is concretized and realized as a result of the love of God and the love of Jesus for us. Our salvation is a loving relationship with God and not a commercial transaction. There is nothing commercial about love.

I, therefore, reject the idea and the doctrine of redemptive suffering, regarding Jesus' salvation ministry, in favor of the following kinds of suffering, which in my view are all relevant to and revealing towards a better understanding of the meaning and the impact of Jesus' suffering.

Corrective Suffering

Corrective Suffering is a kind of suffering that can assist the rehabilitation of a person or persons and help to restore them to a previous condition of well-being or move them to a perspective and commitment toward well-being that is free from error in their thinking and behaviors.

Didactic Suffering

Didactic Suffering is "instructive suffering" that enlightens us. It is suffering that teaches us and others an important lesson or lessons about something considered to be important in the interest of our wholeness and well-being.

Teleological Suffering

Teleological Suffering is "purposeful suffering." It is a kind of suffering that operates toward the realization or the fulfillment of a particular ultimate goal or end. When we read the Gospels, it is clear that Jesus understood His suffering (emotional and physical/anticipated and actual) to be a part of the teleological process having to do with the fulfillment of the ultimate goal of His mission and ministry. See Matt 16:21, Luke 9:22 and 17:25, and John 12:27 and 19:10–11.

Moral Suffering

Moral Suffering is "voluntary suffering" for a cause considered to be just and right for the benefit of humanity as a whole. The adverse consequences of standing up for what one perceives to be just and morally correct often requires moral suffering or suffering for a moral cause. For example, people sometimes go on a hunger strike to protest a moral evil. There are those like Dr. Martin Luther King Jr. who subject themselves to imprisonment while protesting a moral evil. Some moral suffering may require the death of the person or persons concerned, physical torture, imprisonment, or fines, and sometimes the abandonment of family members and friends.

Healing Suffering

Healing Suffering is a kind of suffering that one endures for the well-being of another person or others. It ensues and is realized when a person, for example, gives up a part of their body towards the healing of someone else. This is happening quite frequently as millions donate organs, body parts, or bone marrow while still alive to promote the healing of someone else. Hence it is the suffering of a person for the well-being of another or others.

Sacrificial Suffering

Sacrificial Suffering is suffering that is willfully and voluntarily endured for the sake of other persons whose safety, security, and well-being rise to a level of extreme importance and very high priority and moves the sacrificing person to suffer or to die, if necessary, in order to try to realize it for them.

I have considered *all* the ways in recorded history that the institutional church has tried to connote the meaning of the words *redeem* and *redemption*. But it is clear and *crystal clear* that the original meaning of both words is to denote that something or someone has been *bought back*—that something or someone has been *sold* by someone. That is a lousy and terrible way to describe what God has done for humanity through Jesus Christ.

The words *redeem* and *redemption* distort and *cheapen*, to the point of being ridiculous, the loving concern and care, and the willingness of God to extend Forgiveness, Mercy, and Grace to humanity. Because God loves us, God took the initiative, took it upon Himself, to lovingly, graciously, and *freely* provide for us a pathway to reconciliation with Him through the qualitative "whole life" (the commitment, the selflessness, the teachings, the truths, and the life example) that Jesus lived in all of its relevant and pertinent ramifications to inform, inspire, and encourage human beings to readjust and freely accept, respect, appreciate, and commit to God's gift of salvation/reconciliation, as presented and represented in and through Jesus.

It was and is the institutional church that has associated Jesus with the ancient sacrificial system of the Hebrews/Israelites/Jews, which was a horrible concept. To take an innocent animal and kill it to "pay" God for forgiveness and mercy was and is, wherever practiced, an attempt at *bribery*!

Regarding Accidents

Accidents are chance happenings or events that occur without deliberate intent or design. While it is true that many accidents are the result of the incidental actions or chances that people take, many accidents occur as a result of indifference, negligence, or carelessness by ourselves or other persons and by the forces of nature.

However, many accidents just happen with no previous plan, design, motivation, or intent by any particular person or persons. There are also accidents that occur as a result of random occurrences in nature, such as hurtful or fatal impacts on persons from flying objects or falling objects propelled by strong winds, and hurtful or fatal falls by persons on ice formations that were caused by freezing rain or snow conditions.

Even what we call "good luck" and "bad luck," such as winning or not winning a lottery, are best understood to be accidents. Accidents are among the many things we experience in life that we do not understand and cannot fully explain. We simply do not know and cannot know all of the reasons, conditions, circumstances, incidentals, and so on that operate to cause them. They are for the most part unplanned and unforeseen events and occurrences that happen to us all from time to time.

Yet, it is more likely than less likely that many of our accidents operate to facilitate our well-being. Not all accidents are destructive or fatal. That is inclusive of the hurtful ones perceived as bad luck and the more favorable ones perceived as good luck.

In this universe, in nature, and in the social world of human interactions, "freedom" and "chance" operate to assure that accidents will occur from time to time and much more often than we realize. Nevertheless, we can and do rejoice that most of our accidents are not fatal, even though many do cause us to experience some pain, discomfort, and/or inconvenience.

It is suggested here that the "certainty of human freedom" provides for the opportunity and the experience of accidents. It is undeniable that the deliberate and incidental choices and decisions that we make and act upon often intersect with the deliberate and incidental choices and decisions of other persons, thus resulting in accidents. That is not to say that a favorable or unfavorable accident was intended, but only to acknowledge that the intersecting actions and operations resulting from our choices and decisions combined with the choices and decisions of others guarantees the occurrence of many accidents . . . some hurtful and some joyful.

This understanding does not necessarily preclude or deny the reality of God's provisions in our lives notwithstanding our freedom. While God "allows" the results of the accidental process, God does not "cause" the results. God can, however, transform or assign meaning to the results of our accidents in any way God chooses for God's own purposes and ultimately for our well-being. Initially, that is difficult to comprehend; but that is precisely what the wise poet meant when he wrote these words: "His [God's] purposes will ripen fast, unfolding every hour. The bud may have a bitter taste but sweet will be the flower."[3] Put another way, we may say it thusly: the initial result or the "bud" of intersecting choices and decisions by ourselves and others may be hurtful or even fatal at first glance but, over time, may prove to be or prove to have been instructive, informative, or beneficial to ourselves or others going forward in some important way.

In this universe, we simply cannot thoroughly comprehend the blessedness and value of *joy* until we have some experiences of sorrow. We cannot experience the realization of compassion within our hearts regarding others unless and until we experience pain, disappointment, failure, or loss sometime.

3. William Cowper, "God Moves in a Mysterious Way" (1773).

We rejoice when our accidents are evidences of potential or actual good fortune, and we deeply regret when our accidents are evidences of potential or actual harm. Even so, God has a way of utilizing our joys and our sorrows, our pleasure and pain in ways that can further instruct us and reveal to us some important truths, some important lessons and meanings that are best conveyed to us via the accidental processes ignited by our freedom, the freedom of others, and/or the free operations of natural forces.

Among other things, accidents both favorable and unfavorable teach us that all are vulnerable to their realizations in this world. Accidents teach us to be more alert and careful and not to take anything for granted. Accidents can increase within us a spirit of gratitude for particular reasons that are connected to the accident in some way. An example of this occurs when a family of five persons have a fatal accident where two family members are killed but three survive. The departure of the two is mourned, but the survival of the three is celebrated and oftentimes simultaneously.

There are many other examples where joy and gratitude triumph over pain and death resulting from an accident. Someone has correctly suggested that no matter how bad things are or seem to be, it could be much worse. I add to that, "It can also be or become much better in some meaningful way going forward." That can be realized when our adverse accidental experiences become instructive to us. Many of our adversities eventually reveal to us "certain lessons" that enable us to become more thoughtful and cautious and equipped to share our experiences with others who can learn something important and beneficial from our experiences.

Meaningful Presence in Ministry to the Terminally Ill

Interpersonal Dynamics is a method and a process of ministering to and counseling with a person that is predicated upon the intentional proclivity on the part of the minister/counselor to communicate and relate with the person receiving care and counsel on the strength of an authentic "heart-to-heart" and "person-to-person" relationship that can possibly be established and, if so, will provide the best opportunity for the emergence of meaningful communication, communion, and mutuality as both share with each other in the ministerial care/counseling context.

Regarding ministry to the terminally ill, the practitioner of *Interpersonal Dynamics* proceeds from the following view:

The most meaningful and resourceful communication and communion between the minister/counselor and the terminally ill person is best realized if the minister/counselor does not attempt to rely upon the strength or the impact of his or her official clergy credentials, reputation, or the routine and convenient automatic offering of prayers, Scriptures, and rituals in the effort to meet the early unknown but "suspected" needs of the terminally ill person.

The ministerial care/counseling context with the terminally ill person from the point of beginning, and for as long as the relationship endures between the minister/counselor and the terminally ill person, must be established upon the minister/counselor's genuine presentation of himself or herself as an authentic concerned, caring, and understanding person who is there to listen and respond—and *to often be led* by the terminally ill person, while "sharing with them," as they struggle to peacefully and courageously continue their unique journey through fear, suffering, uncertainty, treatment, hopelessness, and hope.

Every positive resource in the character and personality of the minister/counselor and every supportive belief firmly held by the minister/counselor must be available to uphold the goal and to enhance the function and the process of the interpersonal dynamic.

It cannot be overstressed that ministry through *Interpersonal Dynamics* to the terminally ill person *must begin* with the intent of establishing and maintaining, from the outset, high-quality listening and sharing with the terminally ill person and without imposing upon the terminally ill person theological or religious utterances and conversation. The minister/counselor should patiently rely upon the terminally ill person to voluntarily send a clear signal to the minister/counselor that religious or spiritual dialogue, Scripture, and/or prayer is desirable or needed. This assumes, of course, that the terminally ill person can convey that signal in some way that can be understood.

The practitioner of *Interpersonal Dynamics* should be able to see, as the process unfolds and upon reflection, that this method of person-to-person and heart-to-heart communication can ignite a genuine religious and spiritual experience between himself or herself with the terminally ill person that is authentic communion and thusly more meaningful than the routine "official performance of duty" that is too often the mainstay of ministry to persons who are terminally ill.

III.D — The Nature of Evil, Judgment, and Divine Justice

Regarding Possibility, Opportunity, and Evil

Possibility and opportunity are, at least, two peculiar and unique realities and realizations that have always accompanied God. Even when God was the only fully realized being, possibility and opportunity were two uncreated, unique entities consistently and continuously available for God's use. When God began to create, possibility and opportunity became necessary and indispensable resources for God's creative initiatives, designs, and operations. They remain unique and necessary resources concerning God's creative initiatives, processes, and goals.

It may be difficult to imagine or conceive, but there was a "when" when *evil* was not. The potential for evil as a reality has always been, but its actual presence in the universe has not always been the case.

God has always had a realization of "goodness" in His being and His character. Moreover, God has always affirmed and committed to goodness as the eternal fundamental value in the systematic designs and operation of His eternal purpose.

Evil became a "reality" and a "real presence" in the universe as result of the dynamics of possibility and opportunity and only after God created human beings and endowed them with the power of "free will."

Take notice that in the book of Genesis, evil did not appear until God made it known to Adam and Eve that they were endowed with freedom to obey or disobey Him regarding "the forbidden fruit." At that point possibility and opportunity operated to allow for the emergence of evil as an alternative to goodness.

So, what value did God see in granting humans the autonomy of free will? God decided to grant free will to all persons because God realized that genuine and authentic goodness in persons could not be imposed upon them or compelled within them.

God additionally determined that only through the utilization of their free will could each person have the opportunity to fully develop authentic and genuine character, solely predicated upon their choices, decisions, and actions and their willful commitment to the values that are essential for the emergence of good character in their being.

How do I define possibility and opportunity, these two uniquely occurring and uncreated realities that have always accompanied God? *Possibility* is the "potential" for something to be (to become a reality). *Opportunity* is the "condition" or the circumstance that provides the convenience and the timing for the necessary emergence of specific possibilities into reality and thus into the consciousness and the experience of persons.

God's decision to grant persons the power of free will to make their own choices and decisions, therefore, necessitated the emergence of evil from possibility to reality as an alternative to goodness.

God did not create evil. Evil had to emerge as a matter of necessity as a "possible choice" and as an alternative to goodness to validate the intent and the function of free will. Without the autonomous freedom to choose, a person cannot possibly realize bona fide "good" moral character. Free will absolutely requires the availability of choices and, if possible, the ability to put into effect the choices that one affirms.

So, what is "evil"? The answer is twofold and set forth this way:

Evil is the negative choice available for our free will determinations *when we consider or debate within ourselves* which values we will embrace, affirm, and commit to in our thoughts and actions. Evil is also the negative expression and the negative distortion of the positive values that uphold the initiatives and the eternal purposes of God.

Regarding a Quid Pro Quo Relationship with God?

Our relationship with God is not, never has been, and never will be a quid pro quo, or a "something for something," relationship. That has been one of *the great distortions* and a flagrant misrepresentation of what is operative in a true, proper, and meaningful relationship with God. Moreover, it has done great harm.

To think that we can bargain or barter with God, or that God will bargain and barter with us, is absurd and nonsensical. Clearly, it is necessary and legitimate that we frequently share our cares and concerns with God. But when we pray and meditate, the inclusion of anything in our prayer that implies or suggests that our promises, our devotion, and our commitments to God are offered to God with the expectation, the hope, or a desire that God "bless" us by giving us in return what we want or understand ourselves to need is disrespectful and insulting.

If our relationship with God is proper and sincere, we will not endeavor to follow God's counsel and instruction because we expect God to yield to our will or to reward us; we will do so because we love God and trust God and because it is just the right thing and a good thing to do. When we are inclined to acknowledge the glory and goodness of God through tangible offerings or submissions, the spirit undergirding our giving must be unconditional self-giving, without our looking to God for anything or expecting anything from God in return.

The giving of monetary offerings to God is not "sowing a seed" or making an investment while hoping and expecting God to pay us back and with interest. Proper and genuine monetary giving is *a tangible acknowledgment* that God is worthy of that which we value and treasure and a sign that we are freely giving to God something that we need or could use for ourselves, but we submit it to the Lord or for the Lord in support of what we believe operates to glorify God as our Creator and our Eternal Father.

Our worship, praise, devotion, and service rendered to God is supposed to be our evidence and our witness regarding our love and respect for God. To give to God or to anyone we love expecting something in return corrupts the gift. To give in the right and proper way is to do so lovingly and freely because it is inherently good and right to do so.

A true, proper, and meaningful relationship with God, therefore, is predicated upon the realization of authentic love and respect for God. It requires us to accept that "God's ways are not our ways." It requires that we trust God no matter what. It is legitimate to inform God about our wants, our hopes, and our needs and to petition God for His response—I repeat, *His response*—but we must never approach God with "strings attached" or view our relationship with God from that perspective.

When Shadrach, Meshach, and Abednego were threatened with execution inside that burning furnace, they said to the king who ordered their execution, "Your Majesty, we are confident that our God is able deliver us from the fiery furnace and from your authority, *but even if not*, we will not comply with your demands" (see Dan 3:16–18). Jesus while in the garden of Gethsemane prayed, "Father, if it be possible let this cup of internal suffering pass from Me" (see Matt 26:39). Hearing no favorable response from God, Jesus then said, "Nevertheless, *not My will but Thy will be done.*" In the heat of his relentless physical suffering and grief, Job realized the strength and the submissiveness to tell God, "Though You slay me, *yet will I trust You*" (see Job 13:15).

III.E — Metaphysical Questions: Life, Being, and Existence

Regarding Life (What Is It?)

Life is the power and the resource that enables an entity to have the ability and the opportunity to be and to become whatever God intended for it to be.

Referencing the "self" or the "self-being" that a person is, life is the power and the opportunity bestowed upon it—our "self"—to experience realizations that enable our self to be who and what we were, to be who and what we are, and to become more than we presently are.

Regarding the life of a person (a self-being), to "live" or to "be alive" is to also have the ability and the opportunity to communicate, interact, and share the content of our self with God and other "selves" in ways that are discernible, understood, and meaningful.

Ultimately, death can and will destroy all physical and material expressions of life and reality. That destruction will include the physical container or apparatus that is associated with our self-being on this planet Earth and in this universe. But death cannot ever destroy the power that life is—*the power that enables, sustains, and perpetuates the living, eternal self-being that we are.*

Regarding the Meaning of Life

Philosophically and theologically, especially, life is more than and not limited to biological and physiological processes, activity, and change; neither is life just a quality or quantity which distinguishes the living from the dead.

Life is the "power" or the "resource" that provides us with the opportunity through which we can engage in processes and activity which enables us to be who and what we are, to become who and what we become, to receive and transmit information, and to communicate and share our personhood with God and others in ways that are discernible, meaningful, and purposeful.

Whenever and wherever we observe an organism we consider to be alive, we do not observe life or the "power" in itself. We only observe the effects of that power on the organism.

III.F — Death, Eternity, and the Hope Beyond

Regarding Death

Death is the constant companion of our physical body and is neither friend nor foe.

Death is at times so intimidating and at times so comforting and consoling.

Death as a concept generates fear; the actuality of death can also relieve fear and pain.

Death has no impact or effect in eternity.

Death is inconceivable and unknown in eternity by all persons except God.

Death can only operate in a condition where there is time.

Regarding the Gates of Hell

Jesus has been interpreted to declare that the "gates of hell" will not destabilize or end the purpose and the mission of the church. There are many biblical scholars, however, who contend that Jesus did not say "the gates of hell," which would have been a reference to evil, but the "gates of Hades," a figure of speech which was a reference to death or, more specifically, the impact of death.

I do not know which translation or interpretation is correct, but I do not believe either concept, the gates of hell or the gates of Hades, included in their scope the adverse potential of *indifference*, *unfaithfulness*, *misinformation*, *disinformation*, or *benign neglect*.

In fact, I do not precisely know all that Jesus included in His concept of the "gates." I do know, however, that each of the behaviors that I cited can generate great harm to the stability of the church, the mission of the church, and the unity of the church, and ultimately threaten the very existence and reality of the church here on earth and in the universe. That is why we, the church, must be as faithful and true and as devoted and diligent as we can be.

Adverse actions and behaviors born of the "free will" of persons are quite challenging to God and to Jesus since God has apparently committed to the operations and preservation of personal free will as an ability granted to all thinking persons, who are thus empowered by God to make their own choices and decisions.

If everyone connected to or associated with the church chooses to be indifferent, neglectful, or unfaithful, and so on, that could possibly strike a fatal blow. But even if not fatal, such behaviors and some others can severely disturb, destabilize, and persistently threaten the mission and purpose of the church.

Regarding Heaven / Eternal Life

By far, most references concerning "heaven" or "the heavens" in the Bible are references to all of creation above the earth. They are references to outer space, including the observable contents of outer space, and in some instances it is a reference to the place where God resides and presides, as it were, over all creation. But these concepts and images are not adequate to provide the formation of a rational, logical, and practical view of what we mean by our proclamations regarding heaven.

Jesus' use of the word *paradise* while on the cross at Calvary is considered by many to be a reference to heaven, but *paradise* (an ancient Persian word) is a reference to a beautiful garden or park, and as such, its metaphorical implications are not helpful towards clarifying what heaven is or how we should conceptualize its content and its impact upon us.

Jesus has given to us the assurance that preparation will have been made to receive us into the life beyond this life when our journey through this present life shall have been completed, but even Jesus' implied reference to heaven as a place where there are many dwelling places does not help us to fully or completely understand what heaven is or where it is. In fact, it seems to be quite clear that Jesus was speaking metaphorically when He said to His disciples, and by inference to us, "In My Father's house, there are many mansions, I go to prepare a *place* for you" (see John 14:2).

While it is generally acknowledged that no one on earth knows precisely where heaven is, or what it is or is "similar" to, nevertheless, I suggest the following for consideration:

Heaven is real, but heaven is not a place and is not a physical situation, condition, or structure. Heaven "is" *eternity*. When our journey here on earth ends and our bodies are retired from active service, our "soul"/"self" will enter into eternity where we will realize and experience the blessedness of eternal life, which is not only life that has no end but that has a special and unique quality, opportunity, and meaning. Our physical existence and our physiological processes will end, but our conscious and self-conscious soul-self will continue and be preserved forever.

All biological bodies die, to be sure, but life does not die. The body is animated by life. It lives for a short period of time, but it is not life, and life does not necessarily reside in the body. Life animates the body. We can surely see the effects of life upon the body, but we cannot see the thing in itself that we call *life*. Additionally, there are some expressions and concepts of life that have nothing to do with animation. Some expressions and concepts of life have to do with one's history, purpose, influence, aspirations, endeavors, values, morals, mission, and so on. Our fundamental concept of life and our definition of life is too physically and too physiologically oriented and stand in need of reconsideration, and probably revision. The soul-self is "the person," and the person is more than and other than the body. The life that "is" our personhood is the life that truly matters.

It is this life that has been created to endure the full implications and realities of eternity. This life in eternity will be a joyful, meaningful, and purposeful realization and experience unlike any other realization or experience that we have ever known in this physical and temporal world.

There are many who want "heaven" to be a perfected, unending continuation of earthly experiences and physical existence in a place somewhere "up above," where persons who "get there" primarily worship and praise

God and are forever happy and "at rest" with no particular cares, purposes, obligations, and responsibilities. This simply makes no sense.

Heaven/eternity bears no resemblance to the physical and material universe and life as we presently experience it here on earth. Even if heaven were a perfected or ideal physical and material reality similar to earth and the present universe, it could not meet the standard necessary to be considered eternal or to coexist with the nature of eternity or the realization of eternity.

Additionally, heaven/eternity will not liberate persons from a sense of duty, purpose, obligations, and responsibilities that are meaningful and of assistance to God in some way, having to do with the eternal unfolding and pursuit of God's eternal purposes. If we lived forever without a meaningful sense of duty, purpose, obligations, responsibilities, and so on, that would be extremely monotonous, boring, unfulfilling, and intolerable.

It is my view that persons in heaven/eternity will not be there just resting or just praising God, and we need look no further than our conceptions and views regarding God to clearly understand this. We affirm God as eternal; the one who always was, is, and will be forever. Does not our understanding of God behold God as the Eternal One who is continually creative, purposeful, obligated, and responsible in ways that matter and in ways that are meaningful?

Surely if that is the truth about God in heaven/eternity, we should expect that our presence and our realizations in heaven/eternity will also extend beyond just being blessed while "at rest" forever.

The Problem of Hell and Additional Concerns Regarding Heaven

Everlasting suffering and punishment in hell, imposed or inflicted upon us by God in response to the sinful abuse and misuse of our free will, seems to be inconsistent with the concept of a loving, caring, understanding, forgiving, and merciful God.

Moreover, a hell with conscious and self-conscious persons suffering "in" it forever suggests that a loving, caring, and compassionate God would also suffer and be discomforted forever by that condition and circumstance. After all, the free will that we tend to abuse and misuse is not a self-made entity by any person. Free will is an ability freely given to all persons by

God. Therefore, God cannot escape God's own responsibility for creating some of the conditions (free will or self-determination) that makes sin or the morally wrong choice possible.

It is clear that punishment and revenge have been and continue to be the routine resources and responses that most human beings rely upon and utilize in an effort to assure that justice is administered to persons who have offended them. Such feelings and ways of thinking and behaving by individual humans and communities of humans regarding justice have been so thoroughly ingrained in themselves that such thoughts and practices as retribution and revenge have been projected onto God as a reasonable standard for God's actions in pursuit of justice, and that is erroneous. But the true goal of justice is not punishment or revenge because the purpose of justice is the correction of offending persons and the providing of the means for the offended person or persons to be made "whole" again. Another true purpose of justice is the correction of adverse conditions and situations within the community that cause harm to others.

Punishment without a strong commitment to "true"/"authentic" justice is solely intended to generate suffering, inconvenience, and sometimes execution. We seem to continually ignore the fact that no person can be "forced" or compelled to be a better person or to do what is morally correct or best as a result of punishment or the threat of punishment. Force and threats can compel compliance with a law or a standard, but that is "obedience" and not the free moral choice and commitment of the person concerned.

The motivation for morally correct attitudes, actions, and behaviors must be freely inspired from within the person and freely realized by that person. Such a person is thus enabled to know that when he or she does what is right, best, just, or fair, it is not because they are forced or compelled to do so but because they are driven by the realization that they *ought to do so* simply because it is right, best, just, or fair and so on.

Everlasting punishment inflicted by God upon persons, therefore, would seem to serve no constructive, rehabilitative, or other meaningful purpose. If that is true, everlasting punishment imposed or inflicted upon us by God or anyone is only *revenge*, and that is not consistent with the righteousness and the character of God. So, how should we interpret and view what Jesus, God's chief spokesperson, had to say about judgment, punishment, and hell?

It is reasonable to assume that to Jesus, punishment by "hellfire" or in a "lake of fire" was hyperbole. Jesus' references to judgment and punishment were really references to one's consciousness of self-condemnation fueled by a profound sense of "moral failure" and "guilt," accompanied by a perpetual sense of "lostness" and estrangement from God.

While some of Jesus' teachings do refer to punishment in hell as a consequence of attitudes, actions, and behaviors fostered and driven by sin, Jesus' references to everlasting punishment imposed by God are quite difficult to understand in the light of Jesus' own dominant moral posture and His teachings regarding forgiveness and love and His teachings that God is "our Father." It is reasonable to assume, therefore, that to Jesus, that judgment and punishment by hellfire or in a lake of fire was and is metaphorical hyperbole. Jesus' references to judgment must be understood in the light of His larger teaching about God. I therefore restate that the judgment is not about God seeking retribution but about the moral and spiritual consequences that naturally follow human choices and actions. Jesus' use of the words hell *and* punishment *have to do with our own self condemnation and the attending torment of* guilt *that impacts our conscience and our "being" as a result of our moral failures.*

We cannot ignore that in the Gospels, a number of Jesus' most powerful and meaningful teachings have to do with His presentation of God as a loving, caring, understanding, forgiving, and merciful Father.

Jesus proclaims to us in the Gospels that God's purpose for Him in the world is to seek and to save lost persons. Jesus teaches us in the parables of the prodigal son, the lost coin, and the lost sheep that God's concerns and care for us is so deep and continuous that God is lovingly available to us, lovingly reaches out to us, and joyfully welcomes us back into the security of God's care regardless of the reasons we find ourselves in a "lost condition."

Jesus also teaches us that if we forgive others, God will forgive us and that we should forgive every person seven times seventy times. That means we should, like God, be inclined to forgive as often as the opportunity is there to do so (especially) if our offender should request it.

We should take notice that Jesus did not forgive and generate mercy for the woman accused of adultery because she "believed in Him" or because she requested it. Jesus just simply forgave her, and on her behalf even pleaded to her accusers for mercy and not punishment or execution.

We should remember that most of Jesus' disciples completely abandoned Him immediately after His arrest, trial, and crucifixion. Yet, Jesus restored their connection and fellowship with Him and welcomed them back to the "mission" even though there is no indication they were required to repent or to ask for forgiveness. Likewise, there is no indication that Saul (Paul), the persecutor of Christians, repented or asked to be forgiven by Jesus before he was "called" to preach and bear witness of Jesus.

While being crucified on the cross and in deep agony, Jesus petitioned and appealed to God in this way: "Father, forgive them; for they know not what they do" (Luke 23:34 KJV). Was that an appeal for God to forgive only those who crucified Him, or was it an appeal for God to forgive us all because we do not realize or understand the full impact and implications of many of our thoughts, actions, and behaviors that are offensive to God and operate contrarily to the expectations of God and the ultimate purposes of God? Surely the latter seems to be the more reasonable intent and scope.

Many persons who try to construct a persuasive and convincing case for the reality of heaven and hell apparently do not consider how long or extensive eternal life or everlasting life will be; and we must honestly ask ourselves, Would a loving and caring God impose a condition of suffering "forever" for a few years of moral failure on this planet Earth?

Just the concept of conscious and self-conscious life that has no end *is difficult to imagine. Additionally, if eternal life in heaven has only to do with peace, joy, and rest forever with no meaningful responsibilities, no purposeful work to do, and no challenges to surmount, even that would seem to be a kind of "boring hell."*

Is it not understood that in heaven/eternity God never "slumbers or sleeps" (see Ps 121:4) and is constantly busy, that God has responsibilities and challenges, that God has purposes, and so on? Those are some of the things that make life meaningful here on earth, and without them, living forever on earth or in eternity would probably be intolerable.

In our prayers, we finite, troubled, and frustrated humans often confront our eternal God and our eternal Savior, Jesus, with many of our problems, issues, and concerns, and we insist upon their favorable response and intervention. We look to them for provisions—material, spiritual, and psychological—to help us meet our needs, and we are confident that they do respond with what they consider to be consistent with God's eternal purposes. This suggests to me that if God and Jesus are busy and "working" in heaven/eternity, it is reasonable to assume that we will also. We will be busy assisting God in the full realization of God's eternal purposes forever.

It is also reasonable to assume that heaven / eternal life is not a place, space, or context only for everlasting praise and worship. Nor is it something akin to an everlasting vacation with nothing to do but relax and rest in peace. If it were so, that would also be difficult to endure forever in a meaningful, satisfying, and fulfilling way. It should be remembered that eternal life has no limit and no boundary, and (to use an oxymoron) that is an inconceivably long, long, long, long, long "time" to only rest and celebrate.

Regarding Depression

I assert that *depression* is the consequence of the inability of a person to accept the realization of his or her mortality and the mortality and finiteness of all entities in and of this world that he or she values and treasures. This realization triggers a continuous and unabated sense of the "temporariness" of all persons and things values and treasured, and translates that realization into thoughts and feelings within the person that generate a self-understanding of personal *worthlessness* (no enduring value), *powerlessness* (inability to fix or change the situation), and *hopelessness* (few to no reasons to expect or believe that there is a way out of the pit of despair other than possibly death itself).

Depression is not always manifested in certain outward forms of behaviors that we call *dysfunction*. Nevertheless, it is present in the thoughts and feelings of the afflicted person, generating inner conflicts, anxiety, and disturbances within that deny the afflicted person the realization of enduring peace (harmony). The depressed person is or becomes an exhausted person who lives a life that can be described as an ongoing struggle to "be" at peace with "the self" that one *is* and not the self that one idealizes or the self others perceive him or her to be.

The realization of one's own mortality and the finiteness and the ultimate termination of all persons and things in this life is the ever present, disquieting, and often unspoken "undertone" that penetrates all aspects of a person's life.

We routinely romanticize life. We desire and strive to develop and maintain hopeful and favorable thoughts and feelings regarding the things and the people important to us that are driven by our imaginations and expectations. Confronting and challenging this desire is the ever-present realization of that undertone—that hum, that buzz, or that static in the background of our existence—reminding or informing us of the certain finiteness and mortality of all persons and things, including ourselves.

I suggest that all persons earnestly desire to control the world in which they oftentimes joyfully live and find it intolerable or unacceptable when the pieces they endeavor to use and that give continual substance and meaning to that world do not fit the puzzle they are trying to resolve, consistent with their vision and their aspirations. Therefore, true and enduring peace becomes elusive, and depression is the consequence.

All persons want positive and meaningful permanence regarding all that they treasure and value but cannot escape the reality that all things in this world, including loved ones, other important relationships, joys and pleasures, successes, accomplishments, and so on, will one day be no more, or no longer have value and deep meaning to us. We know this not only intellectually but existentially. It is a consciousness that pervades the very core of our being.

In an effort to relieve the anxiety concomitant with depression, there are persons who seek intermittent distractions such as sex, entertainment, alcohol, drugs, new cars and clothes, a better job, more money to spend, and so on. Others attempt to deal with it through extended medication intervention and/or professional counseling. There are also some persons who attempt to manage it through simple resignation and surrender to the reality that "it is what it is" and that there is nothing for one to do but accept it. Even so, there remains the "buzz" and the "hum" of that undertone in the background of our consciousness and being, informing us that nothing here in this world is permanent, infinite, or eternal no matter how much we desire or strive to have it that way.

In my view, *as per my definition* of depression, it is unlikely and indeed less likely that young children under the age of twelve experience or struggle with depression.

In spite of the contention of some psychologists and psychiatrists, it simply is not likely.

Young children do experience short-term or brief encounters with sadness, grief, anxiety, anger, disappointment, boredom, shock, failure, rejection, and so on, but in young children, these episodes and occurrences are not what I mean by depression because young children cannot connect these experiences with the realization that the whole of life's journey operates that way until journey's end.

To be sure, young children do not have the facilities within their consciousness and self-consciousness during their early stages of development to process or even realize the lifelong nature of things that adversely impact peace of mind. Therefore, true hopelessness and helplessness in young children is not likely. Young children, as I see it, do not and cannot realize a true concept of enduring hopelessness or helplessness, which is an essential component where there seems to be indications or evidence of depression. In fact, that line from fairy tales—"and they lived happily ever after"—is the whole of life and the expectation view that governs the thinking of most young children.

As Christians, we deal with depression through the employment of our system of beliefs and hope, particularly those beliefs and that hope that is offered to us in the gospel of Jesus Christ, which is also called the "good news." We will not completely displace the undertone of anxiety in the background of our lives as long as we live. That "hum," that undertone, in the background is our lifetime predicament. We, as human beings, are finite creatures living or existing in a mortal and finite world. But, through our earnest and sincere acceptance of Jesus as our Savior (our Rescuer) and the intervention regarding our predicament that is offered to us through His gospel, we can and we often do find the means to realize sufficient peace within that brings significant healing to our inner brokenness and disharmony and precludes or mitigates the serious and continuous dysfunction that often accompanies depression in ourselves and many others.

The Christian will surely agree that this life as we come to know it "is what it is," but to that admission, he or she adds, "It shall not always be what it is" because God is our Light in the dark places of our lives, and God's love for us will eternally uphold our true selves as we continue our journey through this life, no matter what.

We as Christians or church members have failed to take notice that much of our Bible content deals with the human predicament of depression. The biblical *report* regarding the exodus of the Hebrews from slavery in Egypt is not only a report having to do with God's endeavors to liberate them from oppression but depression also.

Additionally, the biblical *story* about Job largely concerns itself with the question "Why do good persons suffer?" Job clearly makes the point in this story over and over again that he did not deserve the limitations and disconcertedness he experienced in his life and that he did not understand any of it. Job even asked, "What sense does it make that I was even born? Why did I not die at birth?" (see Job 3:11). Job, throughout the story, was addressing not only his physical pain, suffering, and grief but his depression, his sense of powerlessness, helplessness, and hopelessness.

We Christians or church members have often failed to objectively understand that many Christian hymn writers were really addressing depression when they penned many songs we sing including, among the many, such songs as "By and by when the morning comes, we'll understand it better by and by"; "Be not dismayed whatever betide; God will take care of you," "The Lord Will Make a Way Somehow," "I Will Trust in the Lord till I Die," "On Christ the solid rock I stand, all other ground is sinking sand," "Hold to His hand, God's unchanging hand," "Precious Lord (take my hand, lead me on, let me stand)."[4] Songs such as these were intended to address our depression predicament, either real or potential, with messages of hope, empowerment, and deliverance provided by God as we struggle and journey onward. Fortunately, they have helped many.

One such helpful hymn I now quote in detail is the following:

4. Charles Albert Tindley, "When Morning Comes" (1905); Civilla D. Martin, "God Will Take Care of You" (1905); Thomas A. Dorsey, "The Lord Will Make a Way Somehow" (1943); African American spiritual, "I Will Trust in the Lord till I Die"; Edward Mote, "My Hope Is Built on Nothing Less" (1834); Jennie Wilson, "Hold to God's Unchanging Hand" (1905); Thomas A. Dorsey, "Precious Lord, Take My Hand" (1938).

God moves in a mysterious way,
His wonders to perform;
He plants His footsteps in the sea,
And rides upon the storm.

Judge not the LORD by feeble sense,
But trust Him for His grace;
Behind a frowning providence,
He hides a smiling face.

Blind unbelief is sure to err,
And scan His work in vain;
God is His own interpreter,
And He will make it plain.

His purposes will ripen fast,
Unfolding every hour;
The bud may have a bitter taste,
But sweet will be the flower.[5]

Another hymn that addresses depression by one struggling with it is the following:

O Thou, in whose presence my soul takes delight.
on whom in affliction I call;
my comfort by day, and my song in the night,
my hope, my salvation, my all.

Where dost Thou, dear Shepherd resort with Thy sheep,
to feed them in pastures of love?
Say, why in the valley of death should I weep,
or alone in this wilderness rove?

O why should I wander an alien from Thee,
or cry in the desert for bread?
My foes will rejoice when my sorrows they see,
and smile at the tears I have shed.

Dear Shepherd! I hear, and will follow Thy call;
I love the sweet sound of Thy voice.
Restore and defend me, for Thou art my all,

5. William Cowper, "God Moves in a Mysterious Way" (1773).

And in Thee I will ever rejoice.[6]

I refer to all these hymns/songs that I have mentioned not to suggest that they are a cure for depression but to demonstrate that they were focused on the torment, the struggle, and the despair that they observed either in themselves or others, and addressed it in their songs. There are songs that encourage all of us to realize that in our limited ability to help ourselves or to change the frustrating conditions of mortality, temporariness, and finiteness, we can still believe and trust that there is One who can help us, One who can give to us strength, and One who can give us the enduring peace (harmony within) that we so earnestly desire but find so elusive as we journey through this life.

I say again for added emphasis that these songs that I have referenced, and many others that I did not, were written to address depression both real and potential from an existential and theological perspective.

I close with this summation:

It would be ludicrous, inaccurate, and a misrepresentation for anyone to conclude that my definition of depression and brief analysis regarding depression is a suggestion that the *fear of death* is the cause of depression. The *fear of death* is not even the major component or issue concerned. It is suggested here, in essence, that depression has to do with the realization of the inability of any person (including oneself) to change or to reconstruct in an acceptable way the mortal, finite, and temporary nature and character of our tedious journey through life in this world.

These realizations do occur in all persons, and when one focuses on these realizations, they generate a self-understanding of powerlessness, helplessness, and hopelessness. No matter how many distractions and other preoccupations and devices that we utilize to escape these realizations, we continue our journey, with the resonance of that "buzz," that disquieting undertone, in the background of our lives informing us that all persons and all things in this life that we love, value, and treasure are temporary, finite, and mortal.

6. Joseph Swain, "O Thou, in Whose Presence" (1791).

We are not pleased with this truth, and we are not truly comfortable with this reality. We wish so very much that we could change or remove it from our awareness and the certain realizations of it that we are sure to experience as we continue our journey here on earth until journey's end.

Depression has more to do with mental, emotional, and spiritual *exhaustion* than sadness. To the person afflicted with depression, this life eventually becomes a journey too difficult to continue, a burden too heavy to bear, and a puzzle where all the available pieces they have do not fit the picture of the life they thought they had or desire.

Regarding End-of-Life Choices (Particularly Suicide and Legal Euthanasia)

On the basis of my conversations and observations recently and across the years, I assert that most pastors, and especially African American pastors, are opposed to suicide, legal euthanasia, and the counseling of persons to consider these actions as a viable or desirable response to the adverse complications accompanying terminal illness, no matter how painful, disfiguring, or stressful such may be to a terminally ill person.

The traditional theological and cultural nurturing of African American pastors regarding the sanctity of life is very restraining and does not easily allow for any advocacy of suicide or assisted suicide.

Additionally, it clearly seems that the theological and philosophical stances of African American pastors developed, affirmed, and upheld across the years regarding the unique prerogatives of God, and their confidence in the enabling and sustaining power of faith and hope, just will not permit them to advocate for the radical intervention of direct suicide or assisted suicide, nor to offer any supportive and encouraging counseling of persons to do so towards that end.

Eternal Life, Its Mystery, and the Limits of Our Language

When we venture into the areas of preaching, speculation, or descriptions concerning the *content* and the *meaningfulness* of eternal life in eternity or heaven, we can be sure of only one thing: we simply cannot do it. The inadequacy and the limitations of our earthly or mundane languages do not and cannot enable us to do so.

No matter how earnestly or sincerely we try, the boundaries and the limitations of our present condition and circumstances in this life usually incline us to suggest that eternal life or heaven is a perfected or flawless copy of the life we presently live or the life we desire to live forever. That may be our belief, our hope, and our expectation, but the dominant physical, temporal, and time-oriented nature of our present life and experiences in this world fails to give us a coherent and comprehensive understanding of the content and meaning of eternal life in eternity. We, therefore, end up merely analyzing and contrasting eternal life in eternity in the context of a more perfected and flawless realization of the life and the world that we presently experience. We seem to intuitively know that the eternal is vastly different and other than the temporal, that the spiritual is vastly different and other than the physical, and that life in eternity is beyond our most joyful, purposeful, and meaningful imaginations, but that is as far as we can go.

Whatever we believe to be the true content and the essence of eternity, heaven or eternal life cannot be interpreted or illustrated through the employment of human words, symbols, and signs. They are irrelevant and just simply do not apply when we attempt to use them in our efforts to define and describe eternal life in eternity.

Even if we could experience the quality of eternal life in eternity (which we call heaven) and return to this world and this life with our recollections of that experience, we would still not be able to describe and express the content and meaning of that experience in ways that any other person on earth could truly grasp or comprehend. That is part of the reason the apostle Paul declared, "No eye has seen, no ear has heard, nor has it entered into the heart of any person all the wonderful things that God has prepared for those who love Him" (see 1 Cor 2:9).

It should also be noted that Jesus made no effort to define or describe heaven or eternal life in a comparative or descriptive way with the life that we live and experience here on earth. If Jesus in the yesteryears or even today used language, signs, and symbols that were truly definitive and descriptive of eternal life in heaven, such would be beyond our ability to comprehend.

We have many reasons to trust that our actual realizations and experiences in heaven or eternity will be the best of whatever it is but will have no similar or equivalent comparatives with anything here on earth or in this universe. Our languages, signs, and symbols utilized here on earth cannot capture, explain, or depict the content, meaning, and purpose of eternal life in heaven. Therefore, they are meaningless and totally inapplicable.

In essence, the content, meaning, and purpose of eternity and eternal life cannot be conveyed in language and concepts that are temporal. That is not only true from a theological or philosophical perspective, but even the sciences and mathematics provide no clarifying or definitive assistance to us in this area because eternal life and eternity cannot be quantified or valued with respect to their reality or meaning using the tools and resources of science and mathematics.

Free Will in Eternity?

Free will is a gift and a major part of the way of life that God has bestowed upon us, and it is a gift that will endure forever. Free will is the condition that provides for the realization of authentic love, authentic goodness, and authentic character and righteousness.

Our freewill choices and decisions alone will not operate to exclude us from the privilege of entering the realm of eternity. Motivation, ignorance, poor instruction, peer pressure, and social and cultural pressure certainly will be factors considered by God's evaluation of us.

Free will shall continue in heaven. However, our transition will immediately move us to voluntarily make an irrevocable eternal decision and commitment to affirm and uphold all values that contribute to the well-being of God and all other persons forever and that shall, forever, be our ultimate priority and the foundation of our self-understanding.

Free will alone is not entirely the problem. It is the misuse and the abuse of our free will routinely, to the extent that we prioritize ourselves and joyfully embrace the distorted values that generate disharmony between ourselves and God and disharmony between ourselves and other persons.

We will retain our free will, but it will be impacted even and ever more persuasively and informatively by the counsel of the Holy Spirit. The Holy

Spirit is not a prosecutor, nor is the Holy Spirit a dictator or commander. The Holy Spirit is a Counselor, Persuader, and Comforter.

III.G — Pastoral and Devotional Reflections

I Believe

I believe that God is my Creator.

I believe that God is my eternal Caregiver.

I believe that God dearly loves me.

I believe that God desires my love and respect.

I believe that Jesus is God's unique and supreme revelation to and for all humanity.

I believe that Jesus is my Savior from the adverse consequences of my sinful condition.

I believe that Jesus is my pathway to proper relations with God and with all persons here on earth.

I believe that Jesus is the way, the truth, and the life.

I believe that the Holy Spirit is my Counselor and my Comforter.

I believe that I am a servant of God and a co-worker with God towards the fulfillment of God's eternal purposes.

I believe that when I leave this world I will safely arrive into the realm and the provisions of eternity.

I believe that I will live with God forever.

I believe that God will love me and include me in His goals and purposes forever.

Maintaining a Personal Journal of Poetry Through the Impacts of Existential Uncertainty and Anxiety

Purpose

The "Journal of Poetry" is a "self"-initiated resource, constructed by a person who is struggling with an actual extended health issue considered to be possibly or probably fatal or terminal.

The Journal of Poetry can provide that person with the opportunity and the process through which he or she can get in touch with the "meaning of their being" in a way that can be documented, reviewed, and reflected upon from time to time.

If utilized, the Journal of Poetry can usher the person concerned into moments of meaningful encounters with their "self" at a deep and personal level that can generate helpful perspectives and healing within the person concerned, regarding the aloneness, anxiety, and fear that often accompanies the realization of an imminent threat to one's existence.

Whenever the person in this predicament feels the need, or simply desires, to document their experience in the form of a poem that expresses his or her thoughts and feelings as they journey through their unique and specific struggle, they should do so from time to time for as long as they are able to do so.

The title of each poem can be, but is not limited to, one of the following:

"I"
"If"
"Suppose"
"Maybe"
"Just Thinking"
"Sometimes"
"Long Ago"
"My Goal"
"Somewhere"

"There Was a Time"
"Courage"
"Peace"
"Love"
"God Knows"
"Never"
"There Were Times"

While I am sure that the journal concept I am proposing is heavily influenced by an effort to establish the justification and the foundations for the "Meaningful Presence in Ministry," the purpose or goal of the journal is better viewed as a foundation for the emergence of a "Ministry of Meaningful 'Self'-Discovery" at what is probably the most crucial, disturbing, and challenging situation in a person's experience.

It is through the journal that they are enabled to realize, express, document, and concretize "their truth," which will reveal to them and upon reflection remind them of the emergence of their truth in response to their dread. Persons engaged in this journal process can derive much-needed answers to the questions and issues that concern them, such as,

- Why am I here in this situation?
- What can I do about it (the dread)?
- Am I helpless or hopeless?
- Is this truly the end of me (my "self")?
- Is there anyone who can help me?
- What has been the meaning of my life or the meaning and purpose of my "self"?

These encounters of the self with the self more likely than not are experienced by many persons in what I will now call "the predicament." The particular person of concern, however, cannot receive the full benefit of their "self" encounters, analysis, and conclusions because they do not document them in a form of poems that readily and easily puts them in touch with meaningful recollections of their truths.

SECTION IV

LOVE, EMOTION, AND MORAL CHARACTER

Regarding Love

Love is not a decision, and love is not just a powerful emotion or feeling. Love is the inexplicable realization of a distinctly joyful and meaningful welcoming spirit and connection regarding another person or persons that is persistent and happens in realization without one's deliberate cognitive effort.

Love, therefore, is a very unique realization and is especially meaningful as it generates one's own sense of well-being and facilitates authentic concern and care for the other person or persons and is unconditionally committed to the support of their happiness and well-being. Love affirms the beloved as worthy of the best that one is able to provide.

It is important to understand that this thing in itself that we call love is not a decision. Love is a realization that freely emerges in one's consciousness and within one's being in its own way and time. A person can resist acting on the realization of love or responding to it, but once love is realized, that realization cannot be honestly or truthfully denied.

Since love is not a decision, the command to love must be understood as an instruction to conscientiously try to manifest a welcoming spirit toward others that can become foundational to the realization of love for others. If a person is resistant or not inclined to manifest a fundamental welcoming spirit toward others, love will not likely be realized.

Love is not just an emotion. Love is inclusive of emotion, affection, goodwill, devotion, spirit, protection, appreciation, admiration, respect, commitment, self-giving, kindness and care, sacrifice, responsibility, accountability, empathy, compassion, discipline, constructive criticism, and encouragement—individually and more than all of them combined.

Other creatures may evidence some of the above behaviors or tendencies that we interpret to be affection, sympathy, responsibility and commitment, devotion, and so on, but love, from the view of this author, is a specific and unique person-to-person entity made available to human beings to be shared with other human beings toward the fulfillment of God's intent to make human beings in God's own image and likeness.

Agape — Its Meaning as I Understand It

Agape is a Greek word translated as *love*. This concept of love called *agape* is not just a feeling or emotion. It may and probably does include some significant emotion and feelings, but that is not its essence. Agape is inclusive of my definition of love, but it adds to it the realization of "unconditional" and "total commitment" by a person towards the well-being of another person or other persons. That is its distinguishing quality.

Agape informs and instructs those who possess it and are guided by it to deliberately and thoughtfully engage in actions and behaviors that are consistently predisposed and inclined to allow the presence of agape within themselves to become concretized and made manifest through practices and evidences of goodwill, kindness, compassion, respect, caregiving, and self-giving regarding another person or other persons, while not expecting or demanding anything whatsoever in return, and whether it is appreciated or not.

It must be noted, however, as wonderful and exceptional as agape is, that not all persons will be receptive of the agape offered to them or for them, and not all persons will acknowledge, appreciate, or benefit from its embrace of them. The outcome of the agape offered to others is not in our power to dictate or control. It is the expectation of God, therefore, that we only be the channel through which agape is freely realized and allowed to generously flow from us and through us towards others in the sole interest of their well-being.

The Goal and Purpose of Love

In 1 Corinthians 13, Paul does not attempt to define love or to set forth the purpose of love. Paul describes some of the ways in which love manifests itself or some of the ways in which love operates or behaves. While Paul's descriptions are helpful, some specific considerations of the goal and purpose of love can help to further strengthen our understanding of the utility of love.

1. The goal or purpose of love is to facilitate lifelong peace and harmony with God and with other human beings.
2. In this complex, uncertain, and dangerous world, love is intended to provide for the survival of the human species and not just through sexual relations between males and females but throughout all human relations and interactions.
3. Love serves as the resource or energy that God intended from the beginning of human creation to generate and sustain all positive and beneficial thoughts, feelings, and actions that operate to advance and sustain the well-being of oneself and others.
4. Love is the value that affirms and upholds the intrinsic self-worth of all persons and, in its own way, encourages and facilitates their realization of and commitment to the goal and purpose of love.
5. By God's design, love is intended to impact in a positive way, a life-enhancing way, a value-reinforcing way, and a way considered to be good, an essential self-realization and self-understanding that is consistent with God's vision, God's love, and God's ultimate purposes regarding all persons.

Another Thing About Love

You can teach a person about love.

You can teach a person they ought to love.

You can teach a person the value of love.

You can teach a person the necessity of love.

You can describe to a person some of the beauties and wonders of love.

You can teach a person how to say and do things that appear to be loving, but you cannot teach a person how to love.

If love is to be realized in a person's heart, it must be formed by love itself and realized in its own unique way.

Love is inclusive of but more than a special feeling regarding others.

Love is inclusive of but more than goodness and kindness to and for others.

Love is inclusive of but more than care and compassion offered to others.

We should teach that the realization of love regarding God and all persons should be our highest goal and aspiration. But true, authentic, and genuine love can only become realized and concretized in a person's being in its own unique way.

Love Never Fails Whom or What?

In 1 Corinthians 13:8, Paul asserts that "love never fails." Tell that to a mother who dearly and sincerely loves her children and sacrifices across the years to shelter, clothe, and care for them, only to be disrespected and even physically abused by them. Or tell that to a little boy who loved his estranged father and prayed every night for years that his father would come back home and reunite with the family, only to be disappointed over and over, again and again.

To interpret Paul's teaching that "love never fails" literally is meaningless and is simply not true. Jesus loved Judas. Jesus loved Peter. God loved Adam and Eve. God loved Cain. God loved Solomon. However, Jesus' love and God's love for those persons was not potent enough to overcome their free will and the choices and decisions that they made and acted upon. Love did not keep them completely devoted or faithful to God or God's instructions and expectations in every single instance. God has the same problem with us, and we have the same problem with one another. Our love for our family members and friends does not preclude them from making their own choices and decisions, some of which will be deliberately injurious and hurtful to themselves and others.

What we can and should interpret Paul to mean in 1 Cor 13:8 is this: *love never fails to be what it always has been and what it presently is, "our best hope and our best foundation"* for a healthy, wholesome, and harmonious relationship with God and other persons and our best hope and foundation for peace in this world. Additionally, love is our best hope and our best foundation for an economy that is fair and inclusive, and our best hope and our best foundation for a government that is moral and just, and so on.

Regarding Romance

Romance is the realization of a flood of thoughts and emotions predicated upon one's hopeful and expectant imaginations regarding someone, but imaginations that are uninformed by reason, clarity, and practicality.

The concepts of romance and love are often equated and conjoined but should not be. Simply put, love is the unselfish and unconditional realization of a joyful and welcoming spirit toward another person that inspires a commitment to support and enhance the well-being of that person.

Romance is situational, conditional, fleeting, more narrowly and selfishly focused, and is more likely to be void of sincere and enduring commitment toward the well-being of the other person concerned.

Regarding Jealousy

Across the years, a sharp distinction was made between jealousy and envy. Traditionally, jealousy has been defined as the resentful and annoying emotion realized by a person regarding another person or other persons perceived or suspected of being a personal threat to the continuing possession or presence of something or someone that the foregoing person values and treasures for his or her own reasons.

Envy has traditionally been considered an emotion of resentment realized by a person towards another person or persons perceived to "be something" or to "have something" that the foregoing person wants to either be or to have in their possession or realization. Clearly jealousy in contemporary experience, usage, and understanding has evolved to include envy and covetousness in its scope.

From my view and predicated upon my observations of others and my conversations with others, the understanding of what jealousy is to most persons has evolved. Jealousy is not merely the resentment, suspicion, or fear of losing something or someone to another person considered to be a rival. Jealousy is a deep-seated anger, resentment, and anger toward a particular person perceived to be a rival that is concretized in feelings, thoughts, and perspectives convincing them that the perceived rival has something of value or some advantage or is uniquely endowed with something they wish they had and that the perceived rival is not worthy of having or possessing.

I contend, therefore, that jealousy is an extreme manifestation of delusion that is generated by envy. And I will be so bold as to say that there is no known cure for jealousy, and any attempts to cure it only strengthens and deepens it. By that I mean when one party becomes jealous of another party, the enduring consequence of that party's controlling jealousy is the death of any possibility of a genuine welcoming spirit and wholesome relationship ever between the two parties concerned from that moment onward.

Hatred (an extreme form of anger and hostility) is not necessarily inclusive of jealousy but does often accompany it. Jealously is not hatred. It is an emotional condition that is inclusive of an extreme form of covetousness, selfishness, possessiveness, obsessiveness, and hatred. Therefore, it is reasonable to conclude that jealously is even more enduring and dangerous than hatred. One may, at times, have some success in trying to reason with someone who hates concerning their hatred, but trying to successfully reason with a jealous person regarding their jealousy is doomed to fail.

In all my years, I have *never* witnessed even one case where jealousy was resolved to the extent that an authentic healthy and wholesome relationship eventually emerged between a jealous person and the other person or persons concerned.

The only way to deal effectively with one's potential to become jealous of someone is to thwart or preclude its firm establishment in one's thoughts and feelings upon the earliest recognition of its urge to emerge, and resist it. Once the choice or the decision is made to willingly accept and legitimatize the presence of jealousy into one's being, its presence, at that point, is firmly established, and it is there to stay.

There is much insight and many valuable lessons to be learned from the story of Cain and Abel given to us in the Scriptures by the ancient sages regarding the radical and the extreme impacts of jealousy on human relationships.

Regarding Hatred

Hatred or hate is an extreme feeling of anger regarding a person or group of persons accompanied by extreme ill will and very strong tendencies toward hostility. Hatred is also a mindset or a state of mind that hopes for and seeks satisfaction that the source of its agitation and concentration has been or will be severely injured in some way or destroyed.

Hate is often regarded as the opposite of love, but hate is not the opposite of anything. Hate is a "unique thing" standing alone in and of itself. Although it is a rejection of harmony or friendly relations and any desire for peaceful coexistence with the source of its venom, hatred is not the opposite of love. Just as there is no opposite of the color red or green and so on, and just as there is no opposite of "the middle" of something, hatred has no opposite. The true opposite of love is *indifference.*

Regarding Blessings

We should not evaluate or measure our blessings by the quantity of monetary or material acquisitions that we may accumulate or possess. Blessings should be viewed as the opportunity that God gives to us and all persons to be a blessing to God and to be a blessing to the people we are privileged to serve as members of the family of humanity. That does not necessarily mean to bestow upon them an abundance of material or monetary things but to wisely, thoughtfully, and lovingly utilize all of our resources, monetary, material, spiritual, mental, and so on, to impact humanity in positive ways with a view toward strengthening that portion of humanity that we can impact to initially or further behold themselves as persons who were created to be instruments and servants of God.

I am blessed to have the opportunity to preach the gospel, to convey a word of hope to the hopeless, a word of comfort to the bereaved, a word of encouragement to persons who are tired of their struggle and have either given up or are flirting with thoughts of giving up. I am blessed to inform some persons and to remind others that our greatest blessing is "the opportunity" we have to be a representative of God in the world/universe and to be a blessing to others.

God has given to me the opportunity to realize and utilize such resources that I have as my evidences of my loving-kindness, sharing, caring, forgiveness, fairness, humility, wisdom, understanding, compassion and sympathy, my commitment to true justice, and so on in order to help facilitate the total well-being of all others who can be "blessed" or more greatly enabled by God through me to become the persons God would have them to be.

If my understanding of what it means to be blessed is distorted and unsound, the acquisition of an abundance of money and material things will more likely become meaningless and cursed rather than a blessing. If my understanding of what it means to be blessed is distorted and unsound, my proper focus will elude me, thus compromising any actions and effort on my part to use the opportunity granted to me to be the genuine blessing to all others that God created me to be.

The value and deep meaning of the blessings that God provides to me, for me, and through me are not realized in the simple fact that "I am" or in whatever resources I may possess, but in my realization and my embrace of my life as a privileged opportunity to be a co-worker with God in the furtherance of and towards the realization of God's eternal purposes.

Jesus taught that if we would evidence our greatness and the realization or understanding that we are blessed, it is not evidenced in or by the abundance of the things we acquire or possess but in the *opportunity* to use the gift of life we have been given to be a loving and thoughtful servant and a positive enabler in and through our interactions and communications with part of humanity that can be strengthened in a meaningful way by God through us. To succinctly repeat, the real blessing is the opportunity granted us to be a blessing to others.

SECTION V

SACRAMENTS, PRAYER, AND THE LIFE OF THE CHURCH

Regarding the Sacraments

"The sacrament is an outward sign of inward grace"; that, in essence, is one of the most enduring historic and widely used definitions of what is meant by *sacrament*. It is my view, however, that the sacrament is best understood as a ritual *required* by Jesus and practiced by all believers to serve as a perpetual and reinforcing reminder of our commitment to follow Jesus and to rely upon Him for the realization of grace and the truth that provides for our reconciliation and our harmonious relationship with God, which is, in fact, our salvation.

From this view, there are only two sacraments, two perpetual reinforcing rituals, that Jesus commanded: *baptism* and the *celebration at the table of grace*. Jesus anticipated and expected that whenever we observe or participate in these specific rituals, they would become for us and to us enduring and reinforcing reminders of our commitment to lovingly and joyfully embrace Him, His teachings, and His values with confident assurance that our salvation/restoration of peace and harmony with God will be realized and eternally sustained.

The ritual of *baptism*, using any form of water or any method or mode involving water, is intended to convey in a symbolic way that the process of conversion in the individual has begun in earnest and that the "self" of the individual is being submitted and entrusted to the transforming power of Jesus, which is fully potent to liberate the self of all impediments within that would or could preclude the realization of salvation for the individual concerned. The church (the Christian community), therefore, has an obligation to lovingly, concernedly, and graciously assist "the process" to full completion by saying and doing all that the church possibly can towards that end and for that purpose.

The celebration ritual at *the table of grace*, (often called Communion or the Lord's Supper) is intended to symbolically demonstrate our grateful acceptance of the salvific gift of God to us in the person of Jesus Christ. When we consume the bread and wine (grape juice), it symbolically means we are internalizing the contents and the meaning of Jesus' whole life and being. That is inclusive of His love, His mission, His values, His teachings, His sacrifices, His self-giving, and so on towards the realization of our salvation.

Regarding the Sacrament of Baptism

The sacrament of baptism is best understood as a ritual *required* by Jesus and practiced by all believers to serve as a perpetual and reinforcing reminder of our commitment to follow the instructions of Jesus, and to practice the way of living that Jesus expects of us as we continue our journey here on earth each day and until we complete our journey. Through the sacrament of baptism, our Leader, Jesus Christ, assures us of the real presence and the real activity of the love of God, the grace of God, and the truths and values of God that initiate, sustain, and uphold our most meaningful, purposeful, and harmonious relationship with God and with other persons, which is, in fact, what salvation means. It is the confident assurance that we are by God's love and grace restored to our proper relationship with God as we journey through this life into the life beyond this one, in eternity.

If you are sincere as you accept into your heart and into your being the full intent of the provisions offered to you through your baptism, it will become for you an enduring and reinforcing reminder of your commitment to lovingly and joyfully live your life each day going forward in peace and harmony with God.

The church and the Christian community throughout the world upon learning of your baptismal commitment, therefore, will lovingly, concernedly, and graciously assist you towards the fulfillment of your commitment.

Consistent with the need for you to sincerely make your affirmations, your promises, and thereby your commitment, I shall now ask you the following questions:

Do you affirm the reality that God is?

Do you affirm the proclamation of the Gospel of John in the third chapter and the sixteenth verse that says, "God so loved the world that He gave His only begotten Son, that whosoever believes in Him shall not perish but have eternal life"?

Will you rely wholeheartedly upon the grace of God, through the Lord Jesus, for the blessed gifts of salvation and eternal life?

Regarding "The Table of Grace"

What has been traditionally called the Communion table is for me "the table of grace." It is on this table that the meaningful "presence" and "being" of the Lord Jesus, symbolically displayed as bread and wine or fruit juice from the vine, are made available to grateful baptized believers for our acceptance, internalization, and further contemplation as we celebrate the precious gift of our salvation by God through the self-sacrificing life and the self-giving love of Jesus for us.

The Body and the Blood of Jesus

The self-references by Jesus regarding His *body* and *blood* are clearly metaphorical and are not to be understood in any other way.

Jesus' reference to His *body* was His metaphorical way of calling our attention to the significance of His distinct and unique physical and historical presence in the world as a *human being.*

Jesus' reference to His *blood* was His metaphorical way of placing the focus on His *self,* inclusive of the eternal value and meaning of His willful, purposeful, and loving *self.*

Put another way, Jesus' reference to His *blood* was not a metaphorical reference to a biological component of the physiological processes of the human body. Rather, it was a metaphorical reference to the eternal essence and deep meaning of His whole life and His complete life, including His love, His values, His teachings, His purposes, His good works, and His exemplary way of life.

When Jesus calls upon us to eat His flesh and to drink His blood, therefore, He is calling upon us to receive, internalize, understand, embrace, and live out all that He *was* and all that He *is,* toward the realization and fulfillment of our eternal reconciliation and harmony with God, which is *our salvation.*

Jesus' Exemplary Prayer Life

Jesus' exemplary prayer life is undeniable. Jesus prayed often, but let us follow the evidence regarding Jesus and prayer.

Jesus never taught the disciples to pray until they requested it.

Jesus never specifically taught that prayer could promote or provide for healing, or that prayer was the resource to be used for the resolution of every problem or many problems. One of His own prayers was not answered in the garden of Gethsemane to His satisfaction. Before that, when Jesus went back to His hometown in Nazareth, He could perform no miracles there even though He probably maintained and practiced His prayer life. It is not likely that everyone there who sought His help was an "unbeliever." So, let us stop using that as a "cop-out" or as an attempt to explain.

There is little evidence to support the view that Jesus routinely prayed just before or as He healed anyone. He just got it done in many instances. Additionally, Moses, Abraham, David, and so many others did not get their desired outcome as a result of prayer. Some, to be sure, but not all. Prayer alone was never intended to be a substitute for sound reasoning and decision-making. It more often assists that and is not a replacement for it.

Let me also offer to you the following:

It is reasonable to suggest that in Jesus' day, medical science was not as accomplished as it is today and will be going forward. Therefore, Jesus did what He did to address that gap in that day with reference to a few specific cases.

Jesus never advised anyone to *not seek medical attention* from knowledgeable and able physicians. Remember Luke? Luke was a physician, and although a follower of Jesus and one who probably prayed, it is likely he also maintained his medical practice until he retired or transitioned from this universe.

Fact: God has gifted some people who are not Christians, not religious or preachers, with the ability to heal, and it is ludicrous and unhelpful for anyone to teach otherwise. Yes, it is reasonable to assert that God has given the gift of healing to more physicians than preachers. (The arrogance and misleading egos of many preachers, in particular, resist the truth.)

Have some people been healed or assisted toward healing through prayer? Yes, indeed, but more—far more—have been healed by medical professionals. No doubt about it! Further, most people know this to be true, including you!

So, what is the value and purpose of prayer, and what proper perspective shall we offer to the people regarding prayer, which, to be sure, I believe is a valuable resource and practice for all persons?

Regarding Prayer

Prayer is not a "magic formula" that provides for the immediate fulfillment of every want and need a person may have. Prayer is the means through which a person intentionally and sincerely seeks to address God and to commune—"heart to heart"—with God. The purpose of prayer is usually to share one's concerns and cares with God and, hopefully, to connect with God and receive a favorable response from God.

There is no such thing as a required method or a series of particular components that must be included in order for any prayer to be considered authentic prayer. Indeed, it seems that adherence to a rigid or routine method while praying contradicts the very essence of what prayer is. An authentic and sincere prayer may be very wordy or of few words, such as "Thank you," "I'm sorry," "Forgive me," "I love you," or "Help!" If the one addressed is God, it is still prayer. Additionally, authentic and sincere prayer can be communicated declaratively, interrogatively, or both.

No matter how lengthy or brief, *prayer is the authentic and sincere offering of one's thoughts and feelings to God while trusting that God will hear one's prayer, understand it, and respond.* It is well known that God does not and will not respond favorably to all prayers and neither does God respond unfavorably to all prayers. God does what God does and God will do what God will do consistent with God's eternal purposes.

Precisely how or when God will respond to one's prayer is unfathomable and cannot be predetermined. Nevertheless, one must have and maintain confidence and trust that God will respond in God's own way and in God's own time. Properly understood, the true value and meaning of prayer is realized in the satisfaction and the assurance that one has sincerely communed with God, "the One above all others" who *can* and *will* have the last word regarding the person praying and whatever the intent and the content of that person's prayer. Even if God's response to our prayer is favorable, that does not mean that our hopes and expectations will always be immediately delivered to us. God's actions and operations are not governed by chronological time but kairos time. *Kairos* is a Greek word referencing time that means *at the right moment*, or *at the most opportune, productive, or meaningful occasion*. It is God who makes that determination and not us.

It has been wisely and convincingly stated that in response to our prayers, there are times when God is silent for what may be an extended period of chronological time. Nevertheless, in response to our prayers, there are occasions when God says yes, and there are occasions when God says no! There are also occasions when God says *not yet*!

God does, indeed, do what God does, and God will do what God will do. However, God's responses to our prayers and His intentional and deliberate actions regarding us are always consistent with and supportive of His fundamental character of goodness and His eternal purposes, which are rooted and grounded in the eternal realization and maintenance of love and goodness as fundamental and foundational for the values that God affirms and that God is determined to forever uphold.

Regarding Our Task as Preaching Theologians

We, as preaching theologians, must approach our mission and our purposes with the same or an even higher degree of reason, objectivity, and meticulosity as that which is clearly the pattern of scientists, mathematicians, and engineers.

We, as preaching theologians, have the ears, the trust, and the attention of many persons who profess that they desire and aspire to be in harmony and proper relationship with God, as well as in harmony and proper relationship with all other persons and the whole content of creation. To many of these persons, the quality of that harmony and the appropriateness of all their relationships is vital to their enduring sense of well-being and wholeness. Their desires and aspirations in these regards require quality information that provide them with truths and frames of reference that give them trustworthy guidance and confidence. No person can make quality decisions or commitments absent quality information!

Just because much of the subject matter and content that we deal with is spiritual and moral and will not submit to "proofs" in ways that are similar to the proofs of science and mathematics, that does not excuse us from being as objective, truthful, and honest as we can be regarding our conclusions and our proclamations.

We have not been inspired or called to proclaim to the people nonsense and "smooth sayings," no matter how convenient, popular, or familiar it may be. Our goal must always be to deliver to the people (all people) what we earnestly believe is well-reasoned, coherent, and consistent truth. Additionally, we must always remember that "sincere ignorance" no matter how well intended is still ignorance that will be misleading and often be dangerous.

The Necessity of the Pastor?

To point persons in the direction of a personal and positive relationship with the Creator of the universe.

To facilitate within persons beliefs that can provide a firm foundation upon which they can build their lives.

To teach and reinforce the values and the way set forth by Jesus that empower persons to live in harmony with the Creator and with other persons.

To encourage within persons a powerful sense of moral responsibility for their actions and behaviors.

To be present with persons in times of adversity and distress, providing comfort and counsel that are spiritually grounded.

To clarify and amplify the importance and the wonders of love, hope, and faith.

To help persons sanctify the institutions and relationships that they believe to be ordained by the Creator for their holistic well-being.

To uphold and enable persons to reclaim their dignity and self-esteem when they experience failure.

To facilitate within persons a reasonable expectation of eternal life.

A Sermon Is a "Journey"

This is what is meant by a sermon being a "journey":

The text is the announcement from the Word of God to the people that a specific "journey of consideration and concern" is about to begin.

The subject is the "destination of the journey." It suggests where the preacher and the people will be going *in that specific sermon*!

The proposition is "the reason or the theory" briefly stated that establishes *why* the journey should begin or be undertaken and considered either *important*, *necessary*, *urgent*, or *vital* and, therefore, worthy of the consideration of the people to whom the sermon is proclaimed.

The introduction connects the text to the proposition. It establishes the relationship between the text (the Word of God) and the proposition.

Point #1 is the first thing the people need to hear/consider on the journey in support of the proposition.

Point #2 is the second thing the people need to hear/consider on the journey in support of the proposition.

(*Additional points* should all do the same. However, a maximum of three to four points should be sufficient to uphold or defend the proposition.)

The conclusion notifies the people that the specific destination of that journey has been reached and it is now time for them to determine for themselves where they will go from that point forward and what they will say or do with what they saw, heard, learned, or experienced while on the journey.

Note: In the conclusion, the preacher can also freely express how he or she proposes to utilize and act upon all that they saw, heard, or learned while on the journey.

SECTION VI

SOCIAL JUSTICE, CULTURE, AND CONTEMPORARY ISSUES

Regarding Power and Privilege

The practical realization of power and privilege experienced by a few persons is sometimes harmless and possibly even a resource for thoughts and actions that are good and just. In the experience of a few persons, the condition or realization of power and privilege can even be a blessing and functional in the furtherance of the well-being of others.

While this is possibly true for a few persons, it is not the likely result experienced by most persons who acquire or receive wealth and power. Wealth and power are usually intoxicating. They are more often catalysts for the emergence of egomania, megalomania, and illusions of self-deification to some extent in the mind and the personality of rich and powerful persons. At some point within the consciousness of wealthy and powerful persons, their authentic and natural sense of self becomes lost and replaced with a grandiosely distorted image of oneself as superior and invincible.

These symptoms noted suggest a disconnect with reality that is self-defeating or perhaps better depicted as "self-destroying." That is relevant to what Jesus was pointing out to His disciples when He asked them to consider, "What does it profit a person to gain the whole world and lose their soul [self]?" (see Matt 16:26).

Regarding Democracy as We Practice It

All forms of government, regardless of whether they be monarchial, aristocratic, a republic, theocratic, oligarchical, and so on, are flawed to some degree and do not serve the best interest and well-being of all or most of the people.

In my view, beyond the reach of any doubt, democracy as a form of government has been and is still the most practical and useful form of government developed by human beings. That does not mean, however, that it is perfect. In fact, as ideally practical and useful as it has been, it does have some flaws.

When the democratic form of government was adopted in the United States, all citizens eligible to vote were "white men" who were believed to be devoted to the precepts and prescriptions of the Constitution. Initially, diversity of race and feminine interests in the larger population had no impact on the operations of democracy because non-white races and women for years were ineligible to vote.

The voting constituents (all white men) were expected to vote consistent with the precepts, instructions, and values set forth or implied in the Constitution. Today, however, the voting constituency in the United States is inclusive of mixed races and women, but the majority of the voters are still "white persons" (*male* and female) who do not necessarily cast their votes consistent with the precepts, instructions, and values set forth or implied in the Constitution but who vote what they perceive to be in their own interest as the dominant community of persons bound together by "race."

Therefore, a major flaw in the democratic form of government is this reality; the majority voting population bound together by race and voting to elect or enact whoever and whatever is perceived to be in their best interest will consistently dictate the outcomes of all elections and legislation even though other races of fewer populations do have the right to participate in the voting process.

Regarding the "Me Too Movement"

The "Me Too Movement," which called our attention to gross physical, verbal, and sexual disrespect and abuse of women in particular, needs to be more specifically defined if it is to reasonable and fair, and should be renamed the "Beyond the Boundaries Movement."

Human beings are sexually oriented and have always been naturally inclined to mate or to seek a mate. One human being who delights in the attractive qualities of another person and communicates a signal of that recognition is part of how God made the world. This mating process extends throughout the animal, insect, and flowering plant world, and is a crucial part of the process that ensures the survival of the species.

The problem is not that human beings are sexually and affectionately attracted to each other or one another and that they communicate it, but how should the "boundaries" of what is or is not acceptable or reasonable behavior be clearly determined, defined, and enacted or legislated as law, and by whom?

What some human beings consider to be an offense is often considered by other human beings to be a desirable response to certain deliberate signals that they, themselves, are transmitting to others. There is no questioning the fact that this happens and can be very confusing and misleading to many human beings.

It is objectively clear that no human being should consider it a natural right to practice indecent exposure or to commit battery (i.e., to physically touch or handle another human being without their consent and cooperation), and especially in a civilized society where rules of acceptable conduct and behavior have been clearly and objectively established to protect and serve the well-being of all.

The same applies to the using of force, of one's position of authority, or of mind-altering, sexual, and emotional stimulating drugs and substances by one human being on or within another human being to the unawareness of another human being with the intent to acquire involuntary sexual or affectionate gratification from another human being.

Regarding Evangelicals in the United States

Evangelicals by definition are Christian persons whose values, ethics, and mission are grounded in the *evangelion*, a.k.a. the gospel of Jesus. The gospel of Jesus is the good news as represented in the quality of the whole life or the total life and way of life that Jesus lived and taught. Jesus did not and does not instruct His followers to simply preach any and all good news but to *preach and live His gospel.*

If this definition of Evangelicals is on point, there is absolutely no way that the Evangelicals in the United States can make the legitimate case that Jesus would have affirmed or presently affirms the hurtful rhetoric and the social and nationalistic policies of Donald Trump. Jesus' actions, behaviors, and teachings call upon His followers to be welcoming, loving, respectful, compassionate, and just regarding *all* persons and especially the poor, the oppressed, the disadvantaged, and the weak. That is the very antithesis of what Donald Trump is often saying and doing and calling upon his supporters to affirm and defend.

The continuing use of words by Donald Trump bespeaking the denigration of other individual persons and groups of persons is inhumane and mean-spirited and also stands in stark opposition the gospel that Jesus taught and lived, yet Evangelicals in the United States refuse to take a stance that is clearly, properly, and unalterably aligned with the gospel of Jesus.

Evangelicals in the United States today need a new name to signal or suggest their theological stance. Their self-reference to the name "Evangelicals" is a misnomer when viewed in light of their current expressed political views. Their politics expressed and acted upon under the cover of that name is a distortion of what the gospel of Jesus prescribes as evidenced by what Jesus lived and taught and calls upon His followers to affirm, proclaim, and practice.

There are many Evangelicals in the United States today who conveniently, deliberately, and unashamedly accommodate and who boldly try to the defend their glaring exceptions to what Jesus lived and taught as they pursue goals and objectives that harmonize with their narrower and more selfish sociopolitical and economic stance, and that is both shocking and disgusting.

Regarding the Murder at Emanuel AME Church and Continuing Violence and Murder in Our Nation

Among other things to be sure:

People go to church to get a message.

People go to church to get baptized.

People go to church to get reconciled.

People go to church to get married.

But no one goes to church to get murdered.

The outrageous massacre of nine persons at Emanuel AME Church in Charleston, South Carolina, on Wednesday, June 17, 2015, is a most despicable, horrible, and heartbreaking evil deed. But all murder is evil whenever and wherever it occurs and by whomever. All lives do matter.

Our anger and condemnation of that particular evil murderer in Charleston is justified, and our grief is natural and necessary as we struggle to find healing from the shock and the deep distress inflicted upon many of us. However, our anger and condemnations of murderers throughout the nation are not potent enough to change the status quo or to significantly reduce the propensity of individuals or groups who use violence and murder to resolve disputes or to dramatize and amplify their philosophies and ideologies that are surely grounded in intentional evil.

From ages past to this present date, we have consistently relied upon specific restraints on criminal and uncivil human behavior in the community through the imposition of laws enacted by the state or the community concerned.

We are belatedly coming to the realization that while laws may be instructive to some degree, laws primarily command and demand strict obedience and punish violators only after acts of transgression. Laws do not change hearts. Laws do not inspire people to embrace and affirm moral and ethical behaviors that enhance one's own well-being and the well-being of others in the community. Laws only restrict behavior and lead to punishment of those who violate them.

We need a change in direction and a change in strategy as we earnestly endeavor to reduce and hopefully eliminate violence and especially murder from our communities.

If we are to realize any reasonable hope of creating a different and more effective paradigm, we must direct our attention and focus toward the cultivation and transformation of the hearts and minds of persons in all communities in this nation before evil violent deeds are done, rather than being content with satisfaction, retaliation, or punishment after the deeds are done. This is far from being enough to achieve the ultimate goal of harmony, respect, and peaceful coexistence among all persons in the community.

The cultivation and transformation of persons through persistent, consistent, and continuous communication of a new paradigm throughout the community and the nation as a whole can and will help us to realize the transformation of hearts and minds that we so desperately need.

If we commit to transmitting widespread nonsectarian and nonpartisan messages that highlight and amplify positive values, alternatives to violence, the need for harmony and peaceful coexistence, and respect for all persons, it will over time bring us closer to our goal. If such messages are regularly and persistently disseminated throughout our communities and our nation, they will reach the hearts and minds of many, and many lives will be changed.

We have the means to do this. We are only lacking the will to try. We have more numerous and varied communication resources today than ever before to proclaim our values and ideals to all persons in every community, yet we are not using them in this way.

It is clear that we have the ability and capacity to lift up before all persons the sanctity of life and the importance of reverence and respect for all persons at all times. This must be deliberately taught and consistently reinforced if we are to move toward a different and more hopeful future.

We are not using the full aggregate of our available communication resources to address the problem of violence and murder in our country. We must move in a different direction, and we can if we summon the will.

Contemporary Church Dangers

Modern day dangers to churches:

Carelessly blurring the lines between what is spiritual, commercial activity, and not-for-profit purposes and activities that suggest a for-profit motive.

The ostensible monetary and materialistic lifestyles of the clergy.

Forgetting that the church is a mission, a sent body, to proclaim and live the purposes and teachings of Jesus.

Failure to comply with state and federal codes.

Failure to uphold and advocate for its own professed moral and spiritual values.

Taxation and government regulation.

Regarding the Immanent Threat to Humanity

Bioscientists and electronic and mechanical engineers, in the name of "progress," are thoughtlessly and recklessly determined to transform humans into beings or constructs that are either "akin" to machines/robots or "completely" transformed into machines/robots called cyborgs.

A cyborg will be a human who has been transformed from being physiologically, biologically, spiritually, morally, and socially *human* as a result of the implant or attachment of mechanical and electronic body parts internally, including the brain, the heart, and other vital organs such as the stomach, intestines, kidneys, liver, lungs, eyes, and so on. Over time, this realization will operate to *dehumanize* all individuals. That will not be the intent, but it will be the consequence. This is the ultimate *sin* that will destroy the soul and with it, the sense of personhood and the sense of "self" that has served and is intended by God to serve us so as to make each and all individuals human.

Human beings were intended by God to have feelings that matter to them. Feelings are nonverbal sources of information and communication that humans receive within that they are able to interpret and use to help guide them with respect to certain experiences and events in ways that nothing else can.

It also seems to be undeniable that humans were intended by God to have pain. Pain operates as a warning, and pain is instructive. Humans were intended by God to experience disappointment and sorrow. Disappointment and sorrow operate to increase empathy, sympathy, and compassion within humans. The realization of death and the fear of death enhance our appreciation for life and the importance of using the time that we do have wisely and meaningfully.

The issues arising from present efforts to perfect artificial superintelligence take us back to the underlying message of the Tower of Babel story in the Bible (Gen 11:1–9). The message in that story is that most, if not all, persons have never been happy with the way that God made the world or humans. The people of that day, in the story, built a tower that would reach into God's domain where they presumably would take over and change things according to their vision. Many people today think that if they had made a world, the world would be a place where people would not have pain or suffering, not have disappointment or sorrow, neither experience nor have knowledge of death, and so on. Genesis 3:1–24 is also relevant concerning this.

The fact is, practically all humans have a view regarding how they would have made the world and humans. They would eliminate pain, sickness, death, accidents, sorrow, and many other issues and happenings from their creative process—thinking they would be providing for a better world and a better human being, but would they really be making the world better or humans better? Or would they be eliminating many of the things that give us our humanness, thereby, the word what we understand to mean *humanity*.

SECTION VII

PHILOSOPHICAL REFLECTIONS AND MEDITATIVE PIECES

VII.A — Foundational Epistemology and Human Knowing

Knowledge and Knowing

In this world of time and space, our apprehension and comprehension of knowledge comes in "packets" consisting of many fragments and parts. We begin with one piece or one part that we subsequently connect or associate with other parts and pieces and so on that results in our formation and organization of the knowledge we subsequently realize.

In eternity, our apprehension and comprehension of knowledge, including the knowledge or the knowing of other persons, is not dependent on the "packets" process that we experience here in this universe. In eternity all knowledge is immediate, complete, and at once, without any knowledge dependent upon construction by such fragments as the detailed content of our previous memories and experiences in our yesterdays and yesteryears.

To summarize, in eternity we will have direct apprehension and comprehension of all knowledge. All knowledge will be immediately realized and experienced and comprehended as a complete and unified whole. We will behold, understand, and connect with all things and all persons at once, without the step-by-step rational and logical processing that gives us our knowledge in this universe.

It was this realization and conclusion that inspired John in the book of the Revelation to present the Lord as saying, "Behold, I make *all* things *new*" (Rev 21:5 KJV). This is what our forefathers and mothers meant long ago when they sang, "I've got a new name, a new walk, a new talk, and a new home over in Zion." They likewise sang, "It's always howdy in that land [eternity] where I'm bound."[7] They did not mean by these references that there would simply be "no more dying." They could sense way back then that eternity was to be a realization or an experience forever where there is no more, and therefore, no more days and nights, no more yesterdays, and no more tomorrows, and where all knowledge and knowing will be realized in ways that are not impacted by the limitations of time or space.

7. From the African American spirituals "I've Got a New Name" and "Come and Go with Me."

VII.B — Self, Consciousness, and Human Being

Regarding You and Me

When you were a toddler, you had the realization "I am." In your adolescence, teen years, young adult years, and older adult years, "you," with all the changes associated with those stages, maintained that sense that you were "you." Your body has changed in many ways, including your complexion, size, shape, weight, height, abilities; yet, you are still "you."

If you were severely burned in your face or over most of your body or lost all or most of your outward body parts, thus bearing no resemblance to physical features or abilities that were so familiar to you, you would still be "you." You would still maintain your self-conscious sense of "me." Even if you were a person born blind and had never ever seen your body, you would still have a sense of "I am" or a sense of "me" that distinguished "you" from the "you" that others are.

We innately have an awareness that we are not an entity homogenized or blended into the fabric of a whole, but a differentiated and unique person distinguished from all others. My "me" can never be your "me" and vice versa. Therefore, it is clear that my deeper and abiding sense of "me" and your deeper and abiding sense of "you" are not defined by physique, sights, or sounds familiar to us.

"You" and "I" are at all times other than the physical apparatus with which we are associated. It is so clear to me that the "you" that makes you "you" and the "me" that makes me "me" has nothing to do with my looks, the sound of my voice, or the location or the condition of the physical apparatus with which I am associated. "I" am distinguished from that as much as I am distinguished and differentiated from "you." Think about identical twins that have the *same* identical physical features and even identical or very similar mannerisms and so on; yet, the "self" of each is their own unique, differentiated, and independent self.

Additionally, so many times when I am thinking, I have an awareness that I am thinking but without any conceptualization or inclusion of my body as a part of that process. It is just "me" thinking without the association or the accompaniment of a physical image of my body as I am thinking. More frequently than we seem to realize, our thoughts regarding our "self" are abstract rather than visual. By this, I mean that when I am thinking "I" or "me," no visual image of my physical appearance is a part of that process.

That is often the reason that people have some accidents. They get so lost in their thoughts they momentarily forget that their "self" is associated with a body that accompanies them wherever they go or wherever they are in *this environment* . . . in this universe.

Without any deliberate effort, we often process our thoughts and feelings regarding our "me" and "my" without even the slightest reference, reflection, or inclusion regarding the "body" with which we are associated. My "I," my "me," and my "my" are solid realizations of my reality and my presence as a living being—solid realization without the inclusion of any images or thoughts concerning my body in that thoughtful process

Regarding Consciousness and Self-Consciousness

Where does it come from? Is its origin within the brain, or is the brain merely the receiver and processor of it, similar to a television or radio that receives information, pictures, and sounds at a distance and from outside their containers?

When we observe on the television screen pictures of people and so on, we know that what we are seeing did not and does not originate in that "box" that we call the TV. We know that it was transmitted from afar by a broadcasting source.

The broadcasting source sends out information; if the receiver (the television, radio, or in this case "the brain") is turned off, malfunctions, or breaks down, the pictures and sounds cannot be successfully processed, but that does mean that the broadcasting source has malfunctioned or "died." The brain, while in a condition of disrepair, may not at all times receive the information transmitted by "the self" and thus properly process it even though the information from the broadcaster, i.e., "the self," is still broadcasting but to a broken down, damaged, or turned off receiver.

Can it be that your "self" is the broadcasting source from a distance to and through the brain in order to complement and make more functional the relationship of the self with the body in this physical and temporal environment of our experiences until that relationship is ended by the demise of the body? At this point, "the self" which is immortal vacates its finite relationship with this universe in favor of its natural environment, which is eternity.

Regarding the Brain as the Receiver and Processor of Information

When we look at a television screen, a computer, or a tablet screen, the images and sounds that we see and hear do not originate *in* those devices; they are images, sounds, and content processed *through* those devices. The source of all that content is an outside developer or development that transmits, broadcasts, and conveys its information, sounds, and images *through* devices separate and apart from those devices.

Cannot the brain be more properly understood as a particular kind of device through which the content and the information originating from the "self" is processed and conveyed?

In my view, the self is the originator, the brain is the processor, and the body is the actor.

When a TV or radio stops broadcasting, the problem is usually not with the originating source but is the result of a failure in the processor that prevents the information from getting through. Who has not experienced two or more TVs or radios operating in the same house where one ceases to process what is being transmitted to it but the others still continue to receive, process, and convey what the originating source is still transmitting, even though the "processor" malfunctions.

Cannot the self continue to transmit its content and being to the "brain" but, due to some disturbance or failure within the brain, the brain be not able to process the information being transmitted? The failure of the brain (the receiver) to process the information does not mean that no content or information is being transmitted.

VII.C — Reality, Existence, and Being

Regarding Reality

Reality, or "the real," is a reference to a particular and specific kind and type of entity, experience, occurrence, or realization that "is" or "was," even though we cannot prove it, objectively observe it, or quantify it. We have many experiences in life with some entity that is clearly real, but we only have realizations of the impact or the effect of it upon us while never being able to observe the "thing in itself." Among these are the Spirit of God, a message or instruction from God, love, joy, sorrow, enthusiasm, purpose, anger, beauty, fear, and so on.

If I say I had a dream last night and that it was a real dream, I am only saying that my dream was a real experience or a real dream and not that the content of my dream was, in fact, real; but even my experience of having had a dream is not something I can prove was real. Likewise, the love I realize and experience regarding others is real, but although the reality of its presence within me is something known to me and experienced by me as a factual occurrence and realization, my knowledge of its presence as a fact does not submit to proof via tangible or measurable evidence, objective observation, or logical analysis.

The attempt to determine what is real, therefore, must take into consideration the specific kind and type of entity, experience, or occurrence that concerns us, and the tools needed to decide must be designed to be relevant and revelatory regarding that particular subject matter under review and analysis.

Regarding Nothingness: Is There Such a Thing?

There is no pure reality or condition of *nothingness*. When we speak of or make references to what we define or describe as *nothing*, we are suggesting it is a strange part of our experience that is completely and thoroughly absent and empty of anything at all.

I hasten to point out, however, that just our mere reference to what we call *nothing* is a reference to something. That's right, when we make a reference to or speak of *nothing*, that in itself suggests that we have awareness that even *nothing* is *something*. Moreover, *nothing* always implies the possibility of something. It is always pregnant, as it were, with the possibility of *more than it seems to be* and *more than we conceive or perceive it to be*.

Everything "is," but God was developed, produced, and delivered from a so-called condition of *nothingness*. Nothingness is, in some sense, like a canvas, which is the drawing board of an artist, but with no images on it until it is acted upon by something or someone possessing the ability and the resources of an artist who decides to paint images on it. Like the canvas of an artist, nothingness or what we call nothingness is always available and useful towards becoming more than it was and more than it is.

The blank canvas of an artist may seem to be only a sheet of cloth or paper with nothing on it. Yet, the presence and the availability of that canvas provide for the possibility and the opportunity for that canvas to be adorned with many images in all kinds of colors and shapes and sizes and so on.

So, again, there is no condition of actual nothingness or real nothingness, and our mere reference to even the concept of *nothing* is a reference to *something*. Because *nothing* is *something* therefore, it is always pregnant with the possibility and the opportunity to become more than we initially perceive or consider it to be.

Let me assure you that *God*, the one whose personal name is "I AM THAT I AM" (Exod 3:14), was a reality before there was the appearance or the emergence of what we call *nothingness*. God, the great "I AM THAT I AM," is the one and only unique, eternal, and immortal *reality*, the one and only unique and eternal *being*, and the one and only unique and eternal *dynamic* that has always been a reality even before there was *nothing* and also before there was time.

God, the great "I AM THAT I AM" who is still who He was and is still who He is, is the only entity or being who can or ever will be able to say, "I always was, I still am, and I always will be." There has never been a *when* or *where* and there has never been a *then* or *there* in which the great God was not a reality, and there never will be.

We can affirm with a high degree of certainty that after *God's* self-realization, there emerged in the universe, in this order, *nothingness*, *possibility*, and *opportunity*. And *God*, the great "I AM THAT I AM," is the creative power and the dynamo who allowed for the usefulness of those entities, which, thereby, enabled the creation of the universe that we experience and also the creation and realization of our "self."

Regarding "Being"

Being is often defined as existence, but being is not existence. *Being is life*. Being is the power, the activity, and the *process* that clearly and distinctly *operates* to make a thing what it is for as long as it has "being," a.k.a. life. Being, therefore, has to do with a *living* thing.

As far as we can tell, rocks exist, but do not have being. Neither does a car, a hammer, or a rubber band. These and many other things that exist have physical or material features that we recognize *in them*, but they do not have being just because they exist.

A human corpse has all the features of a person that we recognize, but we also recognize that something is significantly different. Being does not reside there, and being is not associated with it anymore.

Regardless of the size, shape, color, and utility of a thing, if it does not have life, it cannot correctly be said to possess or to have being. This is not to suggest or imply that all life is physiological but to say that "being" is a part of something or associated with something that we recognize as a living thing.

The Uniqueness of Our Uniqueness

Not one of us is necessarily better or worse than anyone else, only different. Different not only regarding our DNA, our fingerprints, our measurements, our looks, our complexion, our race, and so on, but totally different and thoroughly unique. We can all experience the same action, event, or condition as all other persons. But while the impact of our experience may be similar or akin to that of all other persons generally, it will not be the same as our particular experience in detail.

For example, two people or two billion people or more can decide to bake a cake, on the same day, at the same time, in the same location, and using the same recipe. But the mental state, the emotional state, the expectations, the value, the meaning, and purposes that are realized in that cake baking process will be totally unique with respect to each and every person participating in that cake baking process before the cake baking begins, while it is in process, and after the process has been completed. No two or more persons ever share or will share or have the same identical experiences or realizations in detail.

Each and every experience that we have, that we have had, and will have is unique. Our history is unique. Our perceptions are unique. How we learn and what we learn from our experiences is unique. We are thoroughly and completely unique physically, mentally, spiritually, emotionally, biologically, morally, and concerning everything else that functions to make us the distinct and unique persons we are. No person's experience equates precisely—or has the same identical meaning, disappointment, fulfillment, and so on—to any other individual's experience. It's not even close. No person can have a truly identical twin or clone. Each person is totally unique.

Language, culture, folkways, mores, laws, and certain human interactions and social situations, to name a few, provide us with an exaggerated sense of likeness while ignoring or de-emphasizing the reality of the total uniqueness of each and all persons.

"That" I Am

"That" I am is initially the "raw material" available for the realization of my innumerable opportunities and possibilities. "That" I am, with the full potential to become more than I started with, is one of the greatest gifts that God has given to me and also to you.

"Who" and "what" I become is and always shall be determined in largest measure by my thoughts, my decisions, and my actions. Who and what I am at any given point in time is contingent upon my specific and unique history. It is a personal history that I am constantly forming. It has to do with the sum total of my thoughts, actions, and experiences up to and inclusive of every moment "I am" and every moment "I become" as I journey through time.

Regarding the Ground

Practically everything made or produced by mankind was brought forth from the ground, either directly or indirectly, and on purpose. This is inclusive not only of the physical or chemical content of the productions but their usefulness also. Housing, medicine, autos, cell phones, computers, paper, eyeglasses, sidewalks, streets, makeup, airplanes, fire, energy, weapons, food, and clothing are all brought forth directly or indirectly from the ground.

God put all of the raw materials, components, and substances that mankind uses to produce things in the ground. God gave mankind the vision and the ability to bring forth from the ground realizations that once never were and for thousands upon thousands of years could not even be conceived.

With all that has been produced, mankind continues producing more and more from the ground. Why, then, is it so difficult for people to know with confidence that they are far more than their eyes can see and that God is quite capable of enabling all persons to actually become more and more and other than what they can presently see?

Paul the apostle was speaking to the certainty of this reality when he said, "Eyes have not seen and ears have not heard, nor has it yet been revealed to the thoughts or feelings of any person all the wonderful realizations that God shall provide to and for all who love and trust Him" (see 1 Cor 2:9).

VII.D — Theological Explorations

Where Did God Come From? — The Origin and the Emergence of God

Where, when, how, and why did God ever originate? Those questions are unanswerable. We can respond to them intelligently and intelligibly, but ultimately, they are questions that are unanswerable, and they are unanswerable for basically two reasons.

First, they cannot be answered because God has chosen not to disclose it. Secondly, even if we were able to observe that process, or if we should become able to actually observe a reenactment of the process whereby God emerged as a reality, we could not express it. Our human language, our vocabulary, our signs, our symbols, and our math could not help us to truly define, describe, or convey to ourselves nor to any person what we observed. We would have no ability to express or interpret the process.

Using the tools and resources of science, we are able to speak intelligently, intelligibly, and persuasively about the process and the origin of the physical things and the physical universe, but in the domain of things that are *real* but not *physical* or *material*, science and math do not apply!

That being said, I do believe that my views regarding "possibility" and "opportunity" have some relevance in my attempt to give a general response to the question that is intelligible and persuasive, although it is still lacking in the details having to do with the specific and unique process of God's emergence into the reality that God "is."

As I set forth in another document having to do with my affirmations, it is my belief that possibility and opportunity have always been. Before anything or anyone, including God, *possibility* and *opportunity* were the dominant "potentials" in the condition of "nothingness."

As a natural part of the interaction between possibility and opportunity, there was and there is something peculiar about that interaction or that "process" where all the potentials of nothingness insisted upon movement from possibility to probability and from probability to reality.

As a matter of "necessity," I believe that God "emerged" as the catalyst or the source necessary to actually "create" or to incidentally "allow" the subsequent emergence of all potential past, present, and future from possibility to probability and from probability into reality, consistent with God's goals and purposes. God emerged from the potential of nothingness as a matter of necessity to creatively, purposely, meaningfully, or incidentally unleash or release all the potentials of nothingness.

This is my view, and I hope some will find it helpful in my effort to offer a reasonable, intelligent, and intelligible response to a question that we cannot possibly ever answer with absolute certainty. That is not a cop-out. I do think that what I have offered makes more sense as a reasonable and general response to the question posed than some of the "non-sense" that I have heard across the years.

Let us be clear, however, that there are other unanswerable questions regarding nonphysical or nonmaterial realities that do not apply to God. For example: Where did death come from? What is the origin of death? To say that the death of someone's body was the result of a gunshot or sickness only tells us that a gunshot or sickness generated the arrival of death within or upon a particular body, but that does not tell us in detail where death came from nor precisely when, how, or why death itself first originated or emerged from the potential of nothingness as a reality in the universe.

Additionally, I ask, What is the origin of the thing in itself that we call love? Where did love come from? We have no answers to the question why, when, where, or how regarding the origin of love. All we know is that it is a realization that emerges independent of our will, our decisions, and our commands.

Where do ideas come from? Where and when did joy become a reality, and what was the process that moved it to emerge? Where did math come from?

Where does sorrow come from? What is the origin of hope? Where did it come from? Where did *you* come from, or where did you originate? That is not a question regarding your biological and physical body, but *you*. What is the origin of your particular "self"—the unique personality and self that you are?

We cannot pinpoint, describe, name, or explain in detail the origin of any of these realities that have no corporeal or physical existence. The fact is, we don't know when, where, how, or why joy or hope or gratitude or peace and so on emerged from nothingness into reality. We can certainly say that "necessity" required them to move from potential to possibility and from probability into reality. But after all the considerations, investigations, evaluations, computations, and so on, no person but God knows specifically or precisely when, where, how, or why they originated or emerged.

I don't think humanity will ever know specifically or precisely all the details regarding the origin of God or the other entities I have cited plus some others not cited, and in fact, we really don't need to know, but maybe, just maybe, we will understand it better by and by.

Some Inquiries Regarding Jesus

On what is called Palm Sunday, Jesus entered the city of Jerusalem riding on a donkey. His presence generated such a public display of respectful acknowledgment and such tremendous excitement that a few persons standing by who were unfamiliar with Jesus asked the question, "Who is this?" (see Matt 21:1–11).

As Saul (who later changed his name to Paul the apostle) travelled along the road from Jerusalem to Damascus, in Syria, he suddenly saw a bright light that beamed down upon him with such intensity that he fell to the ground and heard a voice asking him, "Saul, Saul, why are you persecuting Me?" In response to that question, Saul asked the question, "Who are you?" (see Acts 9:1–19).

I lift up these two illustrations because the answer to each question that some of the people asked, and the answer to the question that Saul asked, was not predicated upon anything that was physically seen by either. Just seeing Jesus with their eyes, or seeing something like a very bright or unusual light, did not reveal to the people or to Saul anything meaningful or important about Jesus.

What mattered most was not what their eyes saw but what was communicated to their spirits—that is, their hearts and minds—about Jesus, or in the case of Saul, from Jesus.

On many occasions, there are persons who have made inquiries of you regarding Jesus. Since you claim to be one of His followers, and since you affirm Him as your Lord, your Teacher, your Redeemer and Savior, there are people who want to know, *Have you met Him? Do you know Him? Do you really believe He still lives?* Just because you have not met Jesus in the flesh, or seen Jesus with your two eyes, is irrelevant. In fact, we do not "know" any person by just seeing their body. We see a "body" with our eyes, but seeing the body with our eyes is not the same thing as beholding, comprehending, or relating to the "person."

We only know persons and relate to persons by what they communicate to us. The *information* that they transmit to us through the various ways in which they present themselves to us, inclusive of something that has either been spoken, written, or done by that person, reaches us as reliable information and thereby discloses or reveals to us "who they are."

Yes, we can identify a "body" through seeing that body, but our realization of the "person" is wholly dependent upon what is communicated to us by the person in some way. The person is thus more than and other than the body.

Jesus, therefore, is real to me and should be real to you also because Jesus still communicates with us. In His own way (including by the Holy Spirit and the Scriptures / the Word) He continues to speak to my spirit—my heart and mind—informing me who He is, what He stands for, and what He wants me to do and be, as well as what He promises to do and to be for me both now and for all eternity.

Remember this: the true representation of a person is not their body or what they look like but what they communicate to us from "within" themselves or "about" themselves. To me, life itself is the ability and the capacity to receive and transmit or process information. We are all only what we communicate to others.

We know Jesus, and are aware of His presence in the universe and in our lives, not because we have physically seen Him but because He still communicates with us.

The song writer said, "He walks with me, He talks with me, and He tells me I am His own."[8] This means, "Jesus journeys with me and communicates with me, assuring me that I am His, and He is mine."

Regarding Jesus, "The Son of Man"

Approximately ninety times in the New Testament Jesus referred to Himself as the Son of Man. In my view, *Jesus* was referring to Himself as the ideal human being. The authentic and genuine representation or the human being that God conceived at the dawn of creation when God decided to create human beings in God's own "image" and "likeness." The image and likeness of God have to do primarily with the capacity of persons to receive, maintain, and reflect God's love, God's character, and God's values and to share in the realization and the processing of God's purposes. It does not mean that we inherit or become incarnated with God's identical "substance" or "being."

Jesus never directly said, "God and I are the same person." Jesus never directly said, "I am the Son of God." Jesus never directly said, "I am the Messiah." When Jesus said, "The Father and I are one," Jesus was saying that He and God were in *complete* harmony regarding God's love, God's character, God's values and purposes. That means, in the strongest and highest realization possible, Jesus understood Himself to be the clearest, the surest, and the most reliable human representation of God's love, God's character, God's values, God's purposes, God's instruction, and God's self-giving that humanity has ever had or ever will have.

The Humanity and Divinity of Jesus

To be born a human being in this universe is the connection and the association of a person's "life"/"being" with a unique and specific biological and physiological apparatus called "the body."

8. C. Austin Miles, "In the Garden" (1912).

Biologically and physiologically, Jesus was born a human being, lived and functioned here on earth as a human being, but became the divine person He is because of God's supreme confirmation and affirmation in response to Jesus' unique realizations, commitment, devotion, and service in support of the purposes of God and the eternal reconciliation of all humanity with God.

Again, Jesus did not acquire divinity or become divine through procreation or propagation in the way that the church has claimed. Jesus became divine consequential to and as a result of His total commitment and devotion to God and the purposes of God, and His total commitment to the eternal well-being of all humanity.

From His earliest self-realization, Jesus submitted and devoted His self, i.e., His life/being entirely to the will and purposes of God in a way that remains unique in all of history. God, recognizing the uniqueness of Jesus and His total commitment and devotion, not only resurrected Jesus from death but uniquely exalted Jesus above His humanness to a "one of a kind" person imbued with divinity, *not as God* but "like God."

To profess these things does not diminish Jesus but distinguishes, clarifies, and enhances Jesus. They also empower and enhance our opportunity for realizations of genuine and authentic respect and appreciation for the "wonder of Jesus."

Regarding God as the Creator of Jesus

God created Jesus, and Jesus was born with the same free will that all persons have. Jesus, however, differentiated Himself from all other persons in that He freely made choices, decisions, and commitments that brought His will and His feelings into *complete* harmony with the will of God and into *complete* harmony with the purposes of God. It is in this way that Jesus became the only begotten, "one of a kind," Son of God.

Is It God Can't or God Won't?

As reluctant as we are to acknowledge it, the fact is there are some things God cannot do. In many instances, it is not because God does not have the power or the ability but simply because God does not have the will to do so for God's own reasons. God's love, God's wisdom, God's ultimate and eternal purposes, and God's own high moral standards always factor and will always factor into God's decisions and actions, including God's responses to us.

Whatever is possible God can do, but there are some things God cannot do. For example, God cannot make a "square circle" or a "round triangle." God cannot erase a person's previous history. God can discount it and forgive us for generating it if God chooses to do so, but God cannot erase our history. Once we say something, it can never be unsaid or unspoken, and once we do something, it cannot be undone.

God cannot make or force us to love God's own self or any person. God can want our love, request our love, and even demand our love, but God cannot force any one to develop or realize such love. In fact, love is an entity that can only be freely realized by each person regarding another person or other persons. Additionally, God cannot impose good character upon any person. While God can force compliance with God-given laws, dictates, directives, and rules, forced compliance is not an indication of the moral correctness or the good character of any person. Good character can only emerge from the freely chosen values, willful decisions, actions, and behaviors of each particular person in the context of his or her existential situation.

More often than not, however, reason seems to suggest that God's decisions, actions, and behaviors have to do with what God will or will not do as opposed to what God can and cannot do.

Nevertheless, no matter what our priorities, desires, or preferences, God's response towards us will be predicated upon God's love for us, God's wisdom, God's ultimate and eternal purposes, and God's own moral values and standards. This means that in every instance, God is looking at a bigger picture and is at all times considering more than we can imagine or realize as God decides and interacts with us.

God's Ultimate and Eternal Purposes

God's eternal purposes have to do with the ultimate triumph of good over all "actual" evil and even the "possibility" of evil. God's eternal purposes also include the expansion, proliferation, and maintenance of all values affirmed and upheld by God throughout the universe and throughout all eternity.

VII.E — Meaning, Mortality, and Reflective Descent

Where Are They?

Both reason and common sense persuade me to believe that there have been and there still are humans born into this world who at birth were completely blind, completely unable to hear, completely unable to talk or communicate by any means, and completely unable to use their limbs. By completely, I mean *absolutely* and *totally* from the moment of birth and going forward until the body dies.

We have never seen them, heard of them, but they were born into this world. Some have survived infancy and continue their existence, but where are they and why is it that we have no direct knowledge or contact with them?

As far as I have been able to determine, there are no public records, no books, no medical or scientific articles or documents in print or on the internet that shed any light on the existence of these humans.

Were they or are they euthanized? Are they secretly sustained in some particular location until their bodies die? Where are they, and what happens to them?

Imagine

Imagine yourself waking up in the morning alone, on an island in the midst of an ocean, far removed from all expressions and manifestations of civilization—no familiar surroundings, no other humans, no animals, or insect life-forms on the land, in the water, or in the air. You are there alone—no electronics, no newspapers, no books, no clocks, no pencils or notepads, no photos, no mirrors or anything to reflect your physical image. You would still be aware that you were alive, and you would still be aware of your "self" and able to differentiate your "self" from your surroundings and whatever may be the content on that island, such as rocks, fruit, trees, grass, and flowers. That is to say, you would still be able to formulate the realization "I am," as opposed to "It is" or "That is" concerning all other things perceived by you.

Early on, memories from your past would greatly assist your thinking processes, but if you remain on that island under the conditions previously specified for a very long period of time, memories of distant past experiences and events would become diminished, seemingly unreal, and consequently meaningless.

Meaningful and enduring memories over a long period of time require sustained reinforcement from a variety of sources, including shared memories between yourself, family members, friends, and others associated with your memories. Relevant photos, letters, voice and video recordings, relevant music, houses, neighborhoods, places visited, and so on would also serve to reinforce and sustain our memory of persons, images, and events known to us in the past.

Over a very long period of time while in complete isolation and without the benefit of sustained memory reinforcement, memories would fade to the extent that you would eventually question, doubt, and dismiss the content that you once considered to be your "real" past experiences.

On that island under the conditions I have described, the concept of aging would probably not be known to you, and if it were, it would not matter. It is also not likely that even the concept of the death of the body with which you are associated would ever be among your thoughts.

You would still, however, retain your "self-awareness," but over a long period of time, you would become a radically different self than the self you once were. Even so, you would still be a self and, more importantly, be your "self" to you.

The Value of Quality Communication in Interpersonal Relationships

Good communication, especially in interpersonal relationships, is the authentic and mutual sharing of one's thoughts and feelings with another person or others and is inclusive of communication content that never operates to diminish the sense of self-esteem and self-worth of the other person(s) expected to receive and respond to the information offered in the communication context.

A good communication process does not deliberately generate or construct barriers of resistance that hinder the flow of communication. It, therefore, requires respect for the person or persons we engage in conversation. It also requires consistent and continuous consideration and evaluation of the goal and purpose of the information that we propose to communicate, along with consistent and continuous consideration of the tone that accompanies what we communicate.

The Contradiction of Belief

The absence of faith is the truest contradiction of belief. This is to say that our failure to act on what we say we believe, and moreover, our failure to daily live what we claim to believe, is a contradiction.

Lending to the Lord?

It has been said by them of old time, "Whoever is kind to the poor lends to the LORD, and will be repaid in full" (Prov 19:17 NRSV). That is one rendition. Another rendition expresses it this way: "He that hath pity upon the poor lendeth unto the LORD; and that which he hath given will he pay him again" (KJV). The Good News Translation presents it this way: "When you give to the poor, it is like lending to the LORD, and the LORD will pay you back."

A literal interpretation of that concept concerning giving to others or helping others makes me uncomfortable. It does so because it suggests that when we do a good deed, when we are helpful to someone in need by giving them money, food, or clothing and so on, God becomes indebted to us

. . . we put God in debt. That is not possible because God is "the Lord," "the owner," of everything. All the resources of the earth and the universe are God's resources, and it is, therefore, impossible to "lend" God what already belongs to God.

We are stewards. We are servants of God, and God has entrusted us with the opportunity to assist Him in the delivery of His resources to further the well-being of others. That is not truly lending to God; it is "serving God" through our self-giving and caregiving. When done in the right way, i.e., with honorable motivation and a loving spirit, our giving to others in need is its own "reward." The reward is in the joy and fulfillment we realize through genuinely and lovingly serving God and others to the best of our ability.

True "giving" is not a bargain or a deal between ourselves and God or between ourselves and any person. True giving is not something done or some service rendered in order to get something in return or to make someone indebted to us. Therefore, when we give expecting some favor or kindness (a blessing) in return, it is not a gift but an investment, a deal, and a business transaction.

In essence, the blessedness of true giving is not in "what" is given but in the *motivation for giving* and the *appropriateness of the spirit* attached to why and how a person endeavors to give.

Jesus' joy and sense of fulfillment and well-being regarding His service and good works was not derived from the adoration of the people served nor from the realization of His resurrection. In fact, His joy and sense of fulfillment was realized and expressed before His death. That became evident when He said, "It is finished." "Father, into Your hands I commit My spirit" (see John 19:30, Luke 23:46). That was Jesus' way of saying, "My opportunity and My self-giving service for My Father and to humanity here on earth have been completed, and I am satisfied. Therefore, Father, I offer My spirit / My 'self,' to you for your consideration and evaluation. This offering is inclusive of all that I am and all that I have lovingly and selflessly done to serve and bless You and others. Do with Me whatever pleases You! Do with Me whatever pleases You!"

SECTION VIII

CALL TO ACTION

Just Thinking

What are the works that we, as Christians, have been called to do?

We are expected to boldly and faithfully proclaim the gospel of Jesus to all persons through our voices and our actions. What is that gospel? It is the information and the instruction that Jesus taught. It is the information and the instruction from Jesus that can give to all humanity its best opportunity to realize peace and harmony with God, and peace and harmony with one another.

The Constitution cannot do this. The current laws of government cannot do this. It is the gospel of Jesus alone that offers to us all that we need to confront and challenge injustice, violence, hatred, and selfishness when they show up in all human engagement and in all human interactions. But if we do not proclaim and teach His gospel, and if we do not live His gospel, we become nothing more than unlit candles in places and spaces that are ruled by political, social, economic, and moral darkness.

As committed followers of Jesus Christ, we are called and challenged to be vocal and active instruments of God. We are, in fact, the contemporary extensions of the ministry of Jesus Christ in this world and to this world for such a time as this.

Still Just Looking Back or Looking Around and Ahead?

A literal interpretation of all Scripture or every passage of Scripture is a disservice to ourselves and to those persons who sincerely desire to be the people of God and persons who belong to Jesus.

If we preachers of the gospel are to serve this present age and our posterity properly, meaningfully, and effectively, we must spend more time and effort faithfully and consistently following the evidence where it leads while utilizing and applying reason and common sense as we consider the evidence.

The gospel that we have been called to preach can and will nourish and sustain the soul of all persons through all the changes that persons will encounter, but we must take great care to deliver undeniable metaphysical truths that are relevant to the human predicament, present and future.

Stuck in Self-Defeating Ways?

Across the years, you have heard me challenge us all to "strive to reach our full potential as persons." I assume that all who have heard me lift this up for consideration understand what I mean. If not, let me briefly clarify. As we endeavor to live our lives, there are three fundamental commitments regarding ourselves that we can make, and they are to be indifferent, to be mediocre, or to strive toward excellence.

This striving toward excellence or this striving to reach our full potential covers all areas of our lives. It has to do with our spirituality, our morality, our thinking, our abilities, our health, our civic-mindedness, our sense of accountability, and so on. And it is intended to give each of us a healthy sense of well-being, joy, and peace within ourselves, and the satisfaction of honorable achievement.

Here in the United States, we hear a lot of talk about realizing the "American Dream." This concept really means to have the benefits of the provisions of the Constitution, and the freedom to develop and use our skills, abilities, and opportunities to obtain property and wealth. In other words, to be better off materially and financially than the poor throughout the world. The realization of our full potential has to do with more than wealth, houses, and lands. It has to do with who and what we are with respect to our spirituality, our character, and our values.

I earnestly believe that each of us has a sacred obligation to God, ourselves, and the community to do all we can to achieve our full potential as persons. It is my view that the realization of our "full potential" as persons is dependent upon the following:

1. A relationship with God that is personal, respectful, and cherished
2. Submission to the teachings of Jesus

3. A firm belief in ourselves and our ability to learn, to effectively compete, and to achieve
4. A natural inclination to respect the God-given dignity of all persons
5. An unyielding spirit of perseverance

The above formula seems so simple and so capable of being done. But it is clear that many persons all around us are failing to become their best selves. The question therefore that must be answered is *why?* I do suggest that many people approach life and live their lives stuck in self-defeating ways. Some of these self-defeating ways in which many persons are stuck include the following:

1. Spiritual indifference
2. Following the wrong crowd
3. Self-doubt
4. Selfishness and jealousy
5. Acceptance of failure as reasonable

If we and others are to straighten out our lives and move our lives into a positive and fulfilling direction in the right way, we must become liberated and abandon the self-defeating ways that prevent that from happening. Our prisons would be less crowded, there would be fewer cases being litigated in the criminal and civil courts, fewer broken homes, less dropping out from schools by our youth, less war in the world, and less poverty and human neglect in the world.

At the same time, there would be more kindness, more caring, more compassion, more respect and fairness, plus more persons contributing in a meaningful way to the common good of all, and all of that to the glory of God.

Regarding Personal Opportunity

Opportunity is the unique and peculiar condition or circumstance that allows for the actual realization of possibilities (that which can happen) and probabilities (that which is likely to happen) if the person concerned is prepared, willing, and able to act on it.

Opportunity is one of the most meaningful resources for any person's use and continually presents its presence to all persons in assorted and unique ways over the span of the lifetime of most persons. Opportunity "appears" to a person as an "invitation" beckoning that person to do something useful, purposeful, meaningful, and satisfying with it.

A person's response to the invitation of opportunity can be positive, negative, or nonchalant. But if a person is willing, prepared, and able to appropriately respond, opportunity can potentially enable such a person to experience a change in his or her life that is usually more fulfilling.

Sometimes the result of one's opportunity is not favorable or honorable. In fact, sometimes the result can be negative and harmful to oneself and others also. An example of this occurred when the opportunity appeared to some willing and prepared scientists who acted on the opportunity that unleashed the power of the atom and, thereby, provided for the invention of weapons of mass destruction. The recent development of opioid pain medications and the addiction and death resulting from it is another example. Effective preparation, nobility of purpose, and a will to do no harm have much to do with the favorable and beneficial outcomes or consequences of a person's response to the invitation extended by opportunity.

There are many who consider opportunity to be the equivalent of "chance." It is my view, however, that opportunity and chance are not the same. There are subtle but important differences. Chance is more thoroughly rigid and random and presents a higher risk of failure no matter how positive and noble the intent and purpose may be by those persons who act on it.

Opportunity is more flexible and is "more greatly influenced" by the extent of the will, preparation, ability, and commitment of most persons acting on it. The risk of failure regarding opportunity is not always eliminated, but it is significantly reduced in comparison with chance. The results of chance are more "coincidental" while the results of opportunity are more "consequential."

Our Christian Witness and Its Future

It truly puzzles me why the institutional churches and we as Christian proponents, both clergy and laity, are not seriously and thoughtfully looking ahead to the future and preparing for it for as long as we live, from a truthful, honest, meaningful, and sound Christian theological perspective.

It is urgent that we do so with a view toward enabling those who come into the world after we have departed to receive what they need in order to personally benefit from our witness, and to further uphold, strengthen, and maintain the relevance, deep meaning and purposes of God, God's Word, and the "Living Word of God," which is the gospel of Jesus, towards the enduring well-being of themselves and all other persons.

If you do not consider this to be urgent, just think about this: right now, the Bible is not revered and treasured by most of the people in the world nor by most of the people in the Western part of the world, including the United States, nor even most people who profess to be Christians. When is the first time or the most recent time you have seen anyone in a doctors' office or a hospital reading or consulting one?

When was the first time or the most recent time that any person going through a crisis or needing a reason to hopeful or to make an important decision informed you about any enlightenment or encouragement they received from reading or consulting the Bible?

Just take notice that the majority of the people in today's world are not members of any church, and the same holds for the majority of persons in the United States. The failure is not in God or the Bible; it has to do with us, the proponents of God, Christianity, and the church, is inclusive of both clergy and laity. The failure is not in Jesus; it has to do with the failure of us, the "proponents," both clergy and laity, to preach and teach the relevance of the Bible and especially the gospel of Jesus to human beings in a thoughtful, honest, truthful, purposeful, trustworthy, and meaningful way.

The institutional churches and the individual proponents of God and Jesus who would be faithful and true regarding the deep meaning and value of the goals and purposes of God and Jesus for all humanity must accept that such can only be realized when the *truth* is faithfully pursued, located, comprehended, embraced, proclaimed, and lived.

Fundamentalism (the preaching and teaching of literal interpretations of most Scripture or all Scripture), the claims of biblical infallibility at every point, the disinformation inherent in the continuation of financial and material prosperity preaching, the implied or actual nationalizing of Christianity, the resistance of many proponents of Christianity to accept many certain facts uncovered by science, and the failure of many proponents to understand and appreciate the deep value, meaning, and purpose of free will and all its implications do not bode well for the future of Christianity, the church, or the Bible.

Think about it. Just two hundred years from today, the Bible will be even less (far less) revered and treasured and seldom read or consulted by the few persons who will have one in their possession or on their computer or other electronic device.

Just four hundred years from today, most human beings will have a biological body part replaced with a prosthetic, or a physiological organ replaced with a mechanical device. Many foods that humans have consumed for nourishment and replenishment for hundreds or thousands of years will be no more and will be replaced with something man-made that has not yet been invented or developed.

Just one thousand years from today, if not sooner, all human beings will be partly biological, electronic, and mechanical. Governmental structures, economic systems, and educational operations will not look like anything we behold today. By then, most humans will live far longer than is presently the case. What is meant by family then will be quite different from what it has meant and means to us today.

Two thousand years from today, if not sooner, the earth will no longer be inhabited by humans and probably not even be inhabitable. Two thousand years from today, if not sooner, it will be crystal clear that humans are not alone in the universe.

Two thousand years from today, bread, sheep, blood, cake, oxygen, candles, ox, figs, nails, books, money, ancient doctrines, creeds, and so on and on and on, just to name a few, will have no practical meaning to or for humans. Therefore, making references to many things in the world of our past and present experiences will generate a disconnect two thousand years from now.

Can you imagine twenty thousand years from today or two hundred thousand years from today and beyond with all the changes that will be realized and impact humans or the remnants of humans so different from ourselves? I cannot conceive it all, but I am convinced that through it all, God will still be God and the teachings of Jesus and the mission of Jesus will still be relevant to the human predicament and the eternal purposes of God. But we cannot use our free will to serve the will of God or Jesus if we remain intolerant, intransigent, irrelevant, selfish, and controlling elitists. If we do not overcome those impediments, we will not faithfully fulfill our mission to humanity.

Jesus said on one occasion in the Gospel of John, "You shall know the *truth* and the *truth* shall set you free" (see John 8:32). I take that to mean we can be set free from the distortions, limitations, misrepresentations, and impediments that I have noted in this and some of my other affirmations.

God's truth, including especially the truth that Jesus "is," is wider, higher, deeper, more extensive, more inclusive, and more encompassing than the narrow, arrogant, self-righteous posturing of any denomination, association, church, or individual.

That truth is eternal. It extends beyond Bethlehem, Nazareth, Capernaum, Jerusalem, Calvary, the tomb, Rome, the United States, the Western part of this earth, the earth itself, and this universe. It extends beyond the past, the present, our life time here on earth, all the time that yet shall be, and for all eternity. It is inclusive of the whole creation of God and operates to bring the whole creation with all its diversity into harmony and peace with God forever, and this is what *salvation* is.

We Can and We Must Do Better

The vast majority of persons in the world who understand themselves to be Christians may receive "sounds good" and "feels good" information by attending worship services, prayer meetings, and Bible studies, but they do not receive the most reliable, clarifying, or supportive information they need to assist them in formulating and developing a sound and consistent theology that answers their deepest and most troubling questions about the deep meaning, purpose, and content of life and the deep meaning, purpose, and content of their lives in particular.

They do not hear the challenging, clarifying, and edifying voices of Paul Tillich, Karl Barth, Rudolph Bultmann, Reinhold Niebuhr, Edgar Sheffield Brightman, Georgia Harkness, and so on. The majority of Christians or would-be Christians receive their information and instruction from pastors and preachers who are, for the most part, joyfully locked inside boundaries of familiarity and convenience that facilitate routine sermons and proclamations predicated upon weak critical reflection and exegesis regarding the Scriptures, some doctrinal misinformation, and cliché.

When subjected to objective critical review and analysis, much of the preaching and teaching that the majority of the people hear today is indefensible and will be unsustainable as humanity continues its journey forward into the future. In the near future new discoveries, revelations, and realizations will be made known to humanity from other branches of knowledge that will discredit beyond any doubt so much of what has been blithely and routinely proclaimed because of the laziness and theological simplifications which are often casually and irresponsibly asserted by many preachers and other proponents of the gospel and other biblical Scriptures presented as the "Word of God."

Preachers and proponents of Jesus must not allow the fear of renunciation and rejection to stifle their search for truth and deep meaning. If the fear of renunciation and rejection should ever compromise or discourage the search for truth and deep meaning, misinformation and, in some instances, disinformation will likely become even more vogue.

The true and relevant gospel of Jesus that should be joyfully preached and taught does make sense and has great value when the genuine effort is made to properly interpret it. But it falls short of strengthening people as it should and could because of the tendency of many preachers and other proponents to merely quote Jesus and Scripture along with accompanying cliché and with historical or popular interpretations that are illogical and inconsistent with reality. It is very important, therefore, that preachers and all proponents of Jesus "dig deeply" and try to uncover and correctly and meaningfully interpret Jesus' teachings and the counsel of the Scriptures.

Preachers and proponents of Jesus cannot justify ineptness or indifference by hiding behind Isaiah 55:8 in which God says, "My thoughts are not your thoughts, nor are your ways My ways" (NKJV). What God has said in that Scripture is true, but it does not mean that people should not make the sincere effort to understand as clearly as possible what God is saying and doing and why. Using that Scripture as a defense to excuse laziness and the inability or the unwillingness to try to fully comprehend the truth and faithfully proclaim it is unacceptable and a disservice to both God and humanity.

It has been approximately two thousand years since Jesus gave to humanity His gospel, and today, many of His preachers and proponents are, in too many instances, continuing to proclaim a literal interpretation and meaning to all His proclamations while ignoring or understating the full implications of His teachings. We cannot go on doing this much longer.

Who in his or her right mind can possibly believe or think that most of what is preached and taught today will be relevant or meaningful to humankind twenty thousand or two hundred thousand years from now? Right now, things are rapidly changing. Medically, sexually, socially, legally, technologically, extraterrestrially, and ecclesiastically, many things are changing fast, and some things are headed for extinction. This has already begun and will continue beyond anything that can presently be seen or imagined.

Additionally, there are right now more instant information resources in the public domain than ever before and with far more credible resources of indisputable and undeniable information and realities to come that refute, challenge, or raise some serious questions about the validity of what is being preached and taught by too many. Liberation from shallow interpretations of the Scriptures and uncritical acceptance of partially faulty doctrines and partially misguided traditions is urgently needed. The preachers and proponents of Jesus must absolutely struggle and make every effort to arrive at incontrovertible truth and proclaim it. If not, most of them will eventually be dismissed as nothing more than devout and sincere lunatics.

That does not have to be the case. I do firmly believe that the voice of God is in the Scriptures and the truth about Jesus and the wisdom of Jesus can be located in the Gospels and revealed through the counsel of the Holy Spirit. But we must diligently search to "connect" with God and Jesus and their truth therein. If we would make the sincere and persistent effort to locate "the truth" by following all of the evidence where it leads and proclaim it, we can prevent the certain adverse outcomes that will surely occur.

We must not remain content to maintain the status quo and ignore the need for a sound and solid interpretation regarding why and how the Scriptures, Christian doctrines, and traditions operate to edify humanity, strengthen humanity, and usher humanity onward towards eternal reconciliation, harmony, and peace with God in ways that make sense to ourselves and to all persons concerned about this, both present and future.

We seem to ignore or not seriously consider that Christianity is in the early stages of its appearance as a spiritual and religious entity here on earth and in the universe, and we are a significant part of its beginning. Christianity is intended and expected to endure forever, and only God's truth offered to us through His words and the "Living Word," which is Jesus, can provide for that. Cliché, hyperbole, illogical and indefensible assumptions, and assertions may be soothing, mesmerizing, manipulating, and even entertaining, but they are more hurtful than helpful, and we, the proponents of God and Jesus, must be concerned about that and strive for "the truth."

The remnants of humanity in some form will probably still be somewhere in the universe for hundreds of thousand years to come (and perhaps billions of years) in conditions and circumstances radically different from anything we can presently conceive. It is, therefore, clear to me that if the preaching of the gospel and the Word of God is to be relevant and meaningful to all humanity going forward, we must strive to be more objective, more precise, and more honest and truthful than we presently are.

SECTION IX

A SERMONIC WORD

STANDING IN NEED OF THE ULTIMATE AFFIRMATION

By Rev. Dr. Robert L. Foley Sr.

Sermon Text: John 19:28

Indulge me to paraphrase the Gospel of John, chapter 19, and verse 28: "Realizing that He had done all He could, consistent with the prophecies set forth in the Scriptures, Jesus said, 'I am thirsty.'" And I want to speak to you from the subject "Standing in Need of the Ultimate Affirmation."

My brothers and sisters, I say to you quite early on here that if our study and our learning regarding Jesus is to be clearly understood, we must approach our efforts to understand them with the certainty that Jesus often used metaphors, parables, and analogies to express His thoughts, His emotions, and His great truths.

Not everything that Jesus said was meant to be taken literally. His words often conveyed a message and a meaning that was superior and more illuminating—more visual than the literal meaning that it often represented.

I am convinced, therefore, that when Jesus said, "I thirst," or "I am thirsty," His reference was not to a need for water but a need for something from God that only God could satisfy.

You know, there are times in life when we sincerely commit ourselves to a purpose or to a mission that consumes so much of our time and energy that it frequently leaves us exhausted.

There are times, also, when we deeply and sincerely commit ourselves to someone or to others whom we love and care about to the extent that we are moved to give to them and for them all that we can in the interest of their well-being. When we to give them a place of priority in our hearts, our thoughts, our plans, and our actions only to discover that we have been misunderstood, only to discover that we have been abused, taken for granted, often ignored and even rejected, that hurts.

And even we in times like that hunger and thirst for some satisfaction, for some peace that comes from knowing that all we have said and done was not in vain.

That is the predicament in which Jesus found Himself, as He reflected with some disappointment regarding the impact—the measurable impact—of His life and His ministry regarding the people of His Kingdom, and especially so as He neared the end of His earthly ministry on Calvary.

Upon reflection and detailed analysis regarding His ministry, Jesus saw no widespread or concrete evidence of the changes and the improvements that He had tried so hard to generate in the hearts, the minds, and the behavior of those whom He loved and served with all of His being and with all of His strength.

And I dare to say to you that as Jesus drew near and ever closer to Calvary, He was extremely tired and disappointed, already suffering greatly on the inside.

And as someone has correctly said, if you think that the bulk of Jesus' suffering was caused by the beatings that He experienced and by the nails that were hammered into His wrists or into His ankles, if that is the extent of the suffering that you think that Jesus suffered, you are sadly mistaken. That was not the source of His tremendous suffering. There were a whole lot of folks who were crucified in the Roman Empire. There were more than just those two revolutionaries on His right and left who were crucified that day, and the process for all of them was the same. But there was something different about Jesus' suffering in that His suffering had to do with His mission and with His purpose—and His inability to see some results. It gave Him true reason to believe that it was truly all worth it.

So, as to some of my evidence to support that, I'll give you about three or four:

John says in his Gospel, "He came to His own and they did not truly accept Him" (see John 1:11). Some did but most did not. Even in His own homeland and among His own people, He was not accepted. The Bible says that only a few would welcome Him and receive Him.

John says, in the seventh chapter at the fifth verse, that even His own brothers did not believe Him. Isaiah had prophesied in the fifty-third chapter of his Scripture that Jesus would be a man of sorrow and a man acquainted with grief, that He would be despised and rejected. And He experienced that—and especially so as He drew ever closer to the end of His ministry on Calvary.

I remember those times when Jesus had to rebuke and chastise His own disciples by saying to them, "Oh ye of little faith, how long must I put up with you?" (see Mark 9:19).

In another instance He said, "Oh ye of little faith, why are you so scared? Oh, ye of little faith, why do you doubt Me?" (see Matt 8:28). That's what He said to Peter. Peter tried to walk on the water; he lost confidence and started sinking.

I recall the ten lepers He healed. I'm talking about where the real hurt was. I think about those ten lepers, and no one else wanted to have anything to do with them. He took time to heal all ten, but only one came back.

Then I recall the five thousand that He fed with five little barley loaves and two small fish. I think about how they responded to Jesus after He had filled their bellies with food—because that also contributed something regarding His disappointment. You see, when most people read this report about the feeding of the five thousand in the Gospel of John, in the sixth chapter, they read where Jesus fed them sufficiently and even had some leftovers. Everybody will shout *glory hallelujah* to hear that He had enough to take care of them plus some leftovers. And they stop reading right there. But if you read on, if you read on in that same report, it is said that after having fed them, Jesus got on a boat and sailed across the lake to Capernaum. And many of those five thousand were still hanging around. They were looking for Jesus, but they didn't know that He had actually gone. They were hanging around waiting for Him. They weren't waiting for Him to preach. They were waiting for Him to deliver some more food. And when they couldn't find Him there, they got on boats themselves and sailed across the lake and searched until they found Jesus. When they found Him, they said to Him, in effect, "You remember, Jesus, how God fed our leader Moses and the children of Israel with manna from on high when they came out of Egypt and wandered in the wilderness. Why don't You show us another miracle like that?" Jesus said to them, "I have not come to merely provide for your material needs, but I have come to provide for your spiritual needs. And I come to tell you that if you would eat of My flesh and drink of My blood, you will receive eternal life." When Jesus said that, they thought He was talking about cannibalism. And they said, "How in the world can this man talk like that? Talk about eating His flesh and drinking His blood?" (see John 6). They did not understand what Jesus was saying; and anytime the book (i.e., the Bible) talks about the body and blood of Jesus, it's talking about the whole life of Jesus, His whole life. Everything that He—not just His body but His whole life—everything that He stood for, everything that He taught, everything that He proclaimed . . . it had to do with His whole life.

So, Jesus was saying to them when He talked about it, and He's saying to you too, "When you eat of My flesh and drink of My blood," He's saying, "If you internalize My life, if you internalize Me, if you internalize My message, if you internalize My truth, you will find in Me the path that leads to reconciliation with God. You will find in Me the pathway that leads to eternal life." And so, my brothers and my sisters, not understanding what He meant, what did they do? They walked away. Practically every single one of the folks that He fed out there that day, when He said that, because they misunderstood Him, they walked away. And the disciples were looking so shaken that Jesus turned to them and asked them, "Will you also go away?"

And only Peter stepped forward to say, "Lord, to whom shall we go? Because You have the words of eternal life" (see John 6:67). Now that may not be what you all want to hear, but that's the way it is. Yes. And so, He goes a little bit later on into the garden of Gethsemane. And what does He say when He goes into that garden? He says, "My soul is sorrowful even unto death" (see Matt 26:38). And what does that mean? He was saying, "I am so disappointed"—and He's serious—"I am so downhearted." "Father," He said, "if it be possible, let this cup . . ." Now, I know a lot of preachers talk about the cup—that He saw the nails in the cup and the spear in the cup . . . That's nonsense. He was saying, "Father, if it's possible, remove this cup of disappointment, remove this cup of downheartedness, and give Me some assurance that You're satisfied with what I have done. Relieve Me of this present hurt. Relieve Me of this disappointment. Relieve Me of this sense of incompleteness and this sense of unfulfillment."

Brothers and sisters, He had been through so much rejection! Do I have a witness here? He had been through so much desertion! He had anticipated Judas's betrayal. He had anticipated Peter's denial. He even enjoyed, to some extent, the celebration on Palm Sunday, but He also anticipated that none of those folk would be there on Good Friday. And they were not. Even His own disciples had gone back to their old occupations. Those who were fishermen had gone back to fishing—just that quickly! You're talking about hurt. He felt just like you feel when you have given your children every ounce of yourself that you possibly can only for them to disrespect you, to reject you. Some of you, you have these men, and you have these women; you do everything for them. Don't dodge me now. When you do all you can and you don't see any change for the better? When you're doing this, you're not doing it to be thanked. You're doing it because it's right. You're doing it for their well-being. But when you have done all you can do and they reject you like that, and they disrespect you like that, and they ignore you—and some of you are going through that right now—it hurts. Jesus—and I'm just about through—Jesus had gone through all of that. But through it all, having done everything that He could do, He turns to the Father. He didn't turn to those soldiers and ask them for any water. And He could have easily done that. He turned to God and said, "I am thirsty. I need a word from You that will affirm Me. You affirmed Me when I was baptized at the beginning of My ministry. You said, 'This is My beloved Son, in whom I am well pleased.' And today," Jesus was saying, "today, Father, I need to be reaffirmed. Although many that I have preached to did not follow Me"—hallelujah—"did not become a part of My community, I need to hear from You. That it's all right." Do I have a witness here? He said, "Yes, I need a word from You. I don't need anybody to come and tell Me thank you," because many of the folks who say thank you simply don't mean it. Do you all hear what I'm saying? He said to the Father, "I need a word from You,"—Lord God Almighty—"I need to hear You say, 'They may not have followed You; they may not have been converted to the extent that You desire, but I've been watching You. I have been upholding You, and I want You to know that I am satisfied with all the work You've done.'" Do I have a witness here who understands what I mean? Great God! I hear Him saying, "All I want to hear from You, Father, is . . . Just tell Me, 'Well done, well done, My Son, My Son. Well done. You've done all that You can do and I'm satisfied.'"

I'm gonna close this thing and go take my seat, but let me tell you this: Some of you have done the best you can do. Some of you, in trying to do the right thing, in trying to be the right person, you've done everything that you know you do. And yet those folks that you have waited for, they turn up their noses, they turn their backs on you, they walk off and leave you. And I believe today. The thing that can fix it is for you to hear God say, "Well done. Well done. Well done. Well . . . Well done. You good and faithful servant. You've fought a good fight. You've run a good race. You've finished a good work. Well done! Well done!" Oh Lord, I wonder today, is there anybody here who wants to hear the Lord say, "Well done"? If you're here, and if you mean it this morning, why don't you wave your hand? If you want to hear Him say, "Well done," clap your hands. Stomp your feet. Let me hear you say yes, say yes, say yes. Yes . . . Say yes. Thank God today. Well done. Well done. Your children, who've broken your hearts, they never come and say, "I'm sorry." But that's all right. Keep on doing the right thing. Keep on being a blessing to them. And trust God to say, "Well done." Do you know Him? Do you know Him? Do you know Him? Oh, you need to know Him. Yeah. He's all right. He's all right. He's all right. He's all right. You may still have to cry sometimes. You may have to toss and turn—sometimes all night long. But He will fix it. He will fix it. He'll make it all right. Yes, He will. He will. He will make it all right.

The Epilogue

Why Easter Matters to Me

Final Sermon Preached by Rev. Robert L. Foley Sr.
—Easter Sunday, April 21, 2019

Sermon Text: John 14:19—"Because I live, you too shall live."

Today is Easter; it is the day that Christians around the world and Christians in heaven pause from whatever they have been doing to acknowledge and celebrate with gratitude that mighty and most meaningful thing that God did, regarding the resurrection of Jesus, after Jesus had been forsaken by most of His family, His disciples, and friends and then brutalized, murdered, and laid to rest in a borrowed tomb.

Easter is a special day, and the people out there in the world and in the churches who truly understand why it is special embrace it as the most significant day of *hope* ever, in the total history of human beings here on earth.

In my proposal to share with you why Easter matters to me, let me admit that Easter as a "special day" has not always mattered to me for the right reasons.

When I was a child, we did not have the wide variety of things that children have today that generate excitement, things that generate amusement and fun. We did not have televisions or portable music gadgets; we did not have money to go to the movies often—even though it only cost a dime. We had no Nintendo electronics, but we did play checkers—chess was a little bit heavy for us.

We mostly played hide-and-go-seek, but after a while we did that so much until it became boring. Then we found out about a game called spin the bottle, and that game never became boring, but it was quite difficult at times to interest enough girls to play that game. And so when we had nothing else entertaining or exciting to do, we just sat around and made up stories to tell.

We surely enjoyed Christmas Day, but when Easter Day came around, that was a big deal also. When I was child, that was the time when I knew I was going to get a new suit and a new pair of Buster Brown shoes. That was also the time when most of the churches sponsored Easter egg hunts. We did not have any cholesterol problems, so we hunted for all the eggs that were available to be found, and we ate them until we could eat no more. So, Easter mattered a lot to us; it mattered a lot to me, but at that time, *not for the right reasons.*

Another thing, when I became a pastor in 1962 and over the next five or six years, I rejoiced at the arrival of Easter because I knew that we would have a big crowd in church on that Sunday. Again, Easter mattered to me at that time, but clearly not for the right reason.

It was only after witnessing the *bodies* of so many dear relatives and church members reposing in their caskets and later lowered in the bosom of the earth in a cemetery. It came home to me in a real and personal way that one day that would be my body in that casket; and someday, the bodies of all the people I have ever known in their caskets!

And I had to ask myself in a serious way, "Is this all there is?" Do we live in these containers for a short time only for them to become disassociated from our self—our soul?—and destroyed?

Was the journey of my relatives and church members worth the sickness and suffering, the ups and downs, the heartaches and disappointments that they went through and that we all go through, only to have it end in a pile of burnt ashes or in a hole in the ground?

Is this all there is? Have we no *hope* for better? Have we no answer to these questions that make sense to us? Have we no persuasive reference point in history that clarifies what we can expect when *this house*, in which we presently live, is no more?

There are many who are content not to ask these questions, and they say to me, "Reverend, I don't see why you should have a problem with this. Does not the Bible say that Jesus was resurrected?"—*Yes, it does!*—"Do you believe it?"—*Yes, I do!*—"So, what is the problem?"

Jesus' resurrection in and of itself is not a problem. The problem is how we typically view the resurrection. Was it a special circumstance and special condition for Jesus only, or does it apply to all of us? I ask that question because of some things Jesus said. Let me remind you of a few things that Jesus Himself said. Do you remember when He told His disciples and other followers, "Do not fear the things that can destroy your bodies but fear the things that can destroy your soul" (see Matt 10:28)? This is to say, fear the things that can destroy *you*!

In our text, when Jesus said, "Because I live, you too shall live," He *did not say*, "Because I am resurrected, you too shall be resurrected." He said because "I live," you too shall "live." And don't forget what Paul the apostle taught in 1 Cor 15:50. Paul taught that "flesh and blood cannot inherit [enter] the kingdom of God" (NKJV).

Paul also taught that it is more preferable to be *absent* from the body in order to be present with the Lord (2 Cor 5:8).

My brothers and sisters, the point that I want you to leave here with is this: we need to stop trying to suggest that the only pathway to eternal life for ourselves is through the process of resurrection. As far as I am concerned, God can provide for us any way God pleases, but I personally would prefer a new spiritual body to house my soul that is suitable and practical to last forever. But the bottom line is this fact: God will do what God will do! And God is logical. God is practical! And from my view it is illogical to think that my mother and my father and so forth will have to wait in a grave or on a pile of ashes for what could be a million years before we are privileged to enter heaven. That simply makes no sense.

Another thing: The resurrection of Jesus was not and is not intended to *prove* to us that there is life beyond this life and that it is physical. I do believe and I do affirm and proclaim that Jesus was resurrected, *but I cannot prove it, and no one can disprove it. And I say to you in all earnestness that it was never done to prove that there is life after death.*

It ought to be just plain common sense that "eternal life is necessarily real"! Eternal life is necessarily real! Because all life is better than death. Where there is life, there is opportunity! There is activity—there is purpose and function. So, I believe in life, because eternal life is better than eternal death!

The death and the destruction of our bodies cannot possibly mean the end of our "soul" or the end of our "self." That would be a waste of God's time and a waste of our time.

Why would God spend His time making us, loving us, caring for us, *providing for us, forgiving us,* and *concerned to save us* if we are only physical containers that end our earthly journey and our relationship with Him, only to end up in a hole or as a pile of burnt ashes?

When God created us, the theological commentators who commented on our creation were quick to point out after the body had been formed from dirt, God breathed into it "the breath of life," i.e., the spiritual life, *and man became a living soul, not a living body but a living soul.* A living spirit—imperceptible to the human eye but more real and more enduring than anything our eye can see and more real than anything our hands can touch!

So, if Jesus' resurrection was not to prove there is eternal life, then what are some of the purposes—and what does the resurrection truly mean?

I close this message by declaring unto you that Easter truly matters to me because Easter (the resurrection of Jesus) is God's certification that the salvific mission of Jesus here on earth had been faithfully and successfully completed to God's satisfaction.

On that first Easter, God's resurrection of Jesus confirmed and certified in a very special and important way that Jesus had not lived His life in vain, that God was satisfied with all that Jesus had said and done and all that Jesus had given of Himself towards the eternal salvation of humanity, and that really matters to me!

Easter matters to me because it gives me hope and gives me confidence that when I transition out of this body at the end of this journey, neither God nor Jesus need concern themselves with giving me the same or a similar physical body. I just want to *be with them in heaven no matter how they want to do that.* And I don't care whether heaven is up there or down there or in there or out there. Wherever God and Jesus are, that is where I want to be.

Easter matters to me because it gives me solid reasons to trust in that promise that Jesus made to you and me when He said, "Because I *live*, you too shall *live*."

And I've got one more thing I want to tell you regarding why Easter matters to me. When I think about Easter, when I reflect on Easter, it *gives me confidence that when this body*, when this earthly house, this earthly container that is associated with myself, shall be set aside by death, I am confident that I will have another house—another container not made by human hands and built for eternal glory.

I, therefore, can tell you with all my heart that one day, and someday after a while and by and by, *yea, though I will walk through the valley and the shadow of death, I will fear nothing.*

Easter is my guarantee that if I live my life, truly saying and doing the best I can do and pursuing whatever it is that Jesus expects of me, my life also will *not* have been lived in vain.

Easter matters to me because it was on Easter that Jesus Christ was fully authorized and empowered by God to cover me and to cover you with His love and grace—*and committed to take good care of us forever.* Don't you remember what He said just before He ascended into heaven? He said, "Lo, I am with you always" (Matt 28:20 KJV). And I say to that, *praise God from whom all blessings still flow!*

AFTERWORD

I have labored diligently to ensure that my father's legacy as a preacher and teacher is preserved because his commitment to God and to the people of God was genuine and pure. He sought to leave his congregation—and indeed everyone he encountered—with a deeper understanding of who God is, of God's love for His people, and of our responsibility to live faithfully in light of that love.

My father, the Reverend Robert Lewis Foley Sr., was translated from time into eternity on April 26, 2019. He did not have the opportunity to fully structure the book he labored on over a number of years. That task was left for me to complete. A voice within my father spoke, and over time he heard affirmations. Through prayer and love, I carefully considered the affirmations he prepared and the purpose that guided their creation.

Reverend Foley felt within his spirit a deep necessity to write *Affirmations* to challenge readers to more thoughtfully consider their individual role in God's eternal purposes. He did not want people to accept at face value the first thoughts or perceptions that came to mind upon hearing a sermon or reading the Bible. He believed that in both instances there should be thoughtful internal reflection—an examination of how what was preached or read might be applied to one's life. His hope was that such reflection would allow readers to determine for themselves whether deeper truths and greater relevance were present, enabling them to better understand the intent and purposes of the Creator and to more fully align themselves with God.

This book explores themes that touch a wide range of issues affecting all of humanity. Reverend Foley sheds light on those areas that invite thoughtful attention as individuals seek to understand God's plan and their own place within creation. Throughout his life, Reverend Foley met people where they were. He understood that every person moves through progressions over time—from childhood to adulthood, immaturity to maturity, and, at times, faithlessness to faithfulness. It was important to him never to reject anyone. He regarded all people as equally worthy of love and respect.

Affirmations presents a solid foundation for readers seeking to understand religion, worship, and the existence, holiness, and righteousness of God in ways that illuminate God's purposes. Reverend Foley speaks candidly on themes such as goodness and evil, faith and belief.

In section II, he reflects on the personhood of Jesus Christ—His humanity, His preaching and teaching, and His embodiment of grace.

Throughout this book there is a natural progression from Reverend Foley's pastoral care to his philosophical reflection. His interest in philosophy shaped his approach to faith and inquiry. He encourages thoughtful engagement rather than passive acceptance. If readers find themselves challenged to discern God's plan for their life, the author has done well.

He believed that seeking harmony with God is always in one's best interest. Seeking such harmony with God is never undertaken alone because God is present with us at all times.

Affirmations is thoughtfully organized around enduring themes that reveal the depth and range of Reverend Foley's pastoral heart, theological wisdom, and lifelong attentiveness to the human journey of faith.

Section III—the most substantial in the volume—stands as a testament to his profound concern for the human condition and his compassionate commitment to the spiritual formation of humanity.

Throughout the book, the reader is gently guided from foundational meditations on belief, truth, and faith into a reverent exploration of the person and work of Jesus Christ, and onward into the lived realities of prayer, the life of the church, moral responsibility, and philosophical reflection. Taken together, these writings reflect a shepherd's care for souls and an enduring desire to help others live with greater understanding, faithfulness, and hope.

It is my hope that these reflections may serve not only thoughtful readers of faith but also, in time, those engaged in theological study and ministerial formation, as a companion in wrestling with the enduring questions of belief, conscience, and vocation.

My father believed that faith requires engagement, honesty, and courage—not repetition alone. Throughout his life, he challenged himself and others to wrestle deeply with Scripture in order to better understand God, their relationship with God, and their responsibility before God. Some reflections in this volume may invite disagreement or debate. They are included not as provocations but as faithful expressions of his lifelong commitment to seek understanding without surrendering integrity. Out of respect for the author, his voice has been preserved fully and without retreat.

Reverend Foley truly loved people and gave the best of himself in all that he did. Having devoted his life to the service of God and to humanity, his presence, voice, and faithful witness will be deeply missed. He died fully believing that God's plan would allow him to continue in service to God in a reality beyond this life—one that is unknown and unfathomable to us now. Scripture reminds us that no one is able to conceive the things God has prepared for those who love Him.

I hold the conviction that after a lifetime of faithful service, the Reverend Robert Lewis Foley Sr. has received the eternal provisions that only God can provide. May his legacy of service, his love for humanity, and his preaching and teaching continue to bless all who are privileged to encounter these pages.

A Tribute to the Reverend Robert Lewis Foley Sr.

You have challenged me throughout life to be the best person that I could be. You taught me what mattered most: loving God, loving others, and loving myself. I have strived to always believe in the value of love, to be consistent, loving, and kind. I am grateful, most of all, for your admonition that if I do those things, whatever else I do, by the grace of God, He will make a place for me. I am forever thankful for your wisdom and counsel, and I am blessed that your spirit is still informing me to this very day.

Lovingly submitted,

Robert Lewis Foley Jr.

and

Barbara Ann Hall Foley, a faithful and effective partner in ministry, now at rest in God's eternal care, whose quiet leadership helped shape a living legacy of service. Her influence was neither public nor self-seeking, yet it was enduring and formative, grounded in steadfast presence, discernment, and grace. The preacher himself acknowledged this truth in 1993 when he said, "Barbara is not a better person because of the preacher. The preacher is a better man because of Barbara."

Appendix A

Hymns and Sacred Songs (Lyrics) Written by Rev. Robert L. Foley Sr.

"Trusting in His Everlasting Words"

Jesus is my source of truth, Jesus is my source of joy,
I'll trust Him and His everlasting word.
He has made my life complete, and it has new meaning,
I'll trust Him and His everlasting word.

I'll trust Him, I'll trust Him, I'll trust Him and depend on Him,
I'll trust Him, I'll trust Him, I'll trust Him and His everlasting word.

Since He came into my heart, I have found such peace and love,
I'll trust Him and His everlasting word.
I know Jesus cares for me; I know that He hears my cries,
I'll trust Him and His everlasting word.

I'll trust Him, I'll trust Him, I'll trust Him and depend on Him,
I'll trust Him, I'll trust Him, I'll trust Him and His everlasting word.

Jesus helps me face my fears, He's my source of hope and strength,
I'll trust Him and His everlasting word.
He has told me He's the way, and He tells me follow Him,
I'll trust Him and His everlasting word.

I'll trust Him, I'll trust Him, I'll trust Him and depend on Him,
I'll trust Him, I'll trust Him, I'll trust Him and His everlasting word.

"Worthy and Bless-ed Is He"

(To be sung to the tune of "We Are Climbing Jacob's Ladder")

I love—and I praise—Jesus my Savior;
I love—and I praise—Jesus my Savior;
I love—and I praise—Jesus my Savior;

Worthy—and bless-ed—is He.

Each day, He makes me stronger and stronger;
Each day, He makes me stronger and stronger;
Each day, He makes me stronger and stronger;

Worthy—and bless-ed—is He.

My life is different, because of—my Jesus;
My life is different, because of—my Jesus;
My life is different, because of—my Jesus;

Worthy—and bless-ed—is He.

If you know Him, why not—praise Him;
If you know Him, why not—praise Him;
If you know Him, why not—praise Him;

Worthy—and bless-ed—is He.

Appendix B

Quotations

Some of My Original Quotations

"If you want to avoid a conflict, don't start one. If someone else starts a conflict, you can choose not to participate."

"No one can ever be truly grateful for something that they think they deserve."

"Food nourishes your body, but love nourishes your being."

"Experience is the tuition that we pay for the lessons that we learn in life."

"*Truth* is the most reliable information that a person can have regarding any question or concern at any particular time."

"Hope is the last light in a person's life to ever go dim."

"Your parents and other persons will teach you many lessons, and some of them you will forget, but you will probably never forget the lessons that you are taught by trouble."

"When you are going through trouble, try to connect with what trouble is trying to teach you."

"Almost everything that we deliberately do or propose to do begins with our imagination."

"You cannot kill time, but you can sure waste time and kill your opportunities to be productive."

More of My Original Quotations

"Faith is more than belief. Faith is what you do and how you daily live, consistent with what you say you believe."

"The smallest good deeds that you actually do are more beneficial and meaningful than all the good deeds you plan to do."

"We are all flawed and stand in need of God's amazing grace."

"When you get very angry, think of the possible consequences if you do what anger tells you to do."

"If God did not want you to be here in this world, you would not be here. So why be here and not try to discover or realize what God had in mind when God brought you forth to be here?"

"It takes more time and energy to pretend to be something or someone that you are not than to simply be yourself."

"There are times when only tears can soothe the hurt and pain in an aching heart."

"If the truth is told, we don't need God because we love God, we need God because God loves us."

"One of the things that God wants each of us to do is help keep other human beings human."

"The clearest evidence of the greater love is seen whenever a person is willing to sacrifice their convenience, their own comfort, and their own security for the well-being of another person."

"If you are depending on computers to answer most of your questions, to supply you with most of your information, to help to think for you and remember things for you, you are making a big mistake."

www.ingramcontent.com/pod-product-compliance
Lightning Source LLC
LaVergne TN
LVHW050624100826
845148LV00011B/1717